KT-471-104

250 480 202

THE ROUGH GUIDE TO
Flute and Piccolo

Whether you're a beginner or a pro, whether you are about to buy a flute or you want to learn more about the one you already have – this book is for you.

Hugo Pinksterboer

THE ESSENTIAL TIPBOOK

Publishing Details

This first edition published Nov 2001 by Rough Guides Ltd,
62–70 Shorts Gardens, London WC2H 9AH

Distributed by the Penguin Group:
Penguin Books Ltd, 27 Wrights Lane, London W8 5TZ
Penguin Putnam, Inc., 375 Hudson Street, New York, NY 10014
Penguin Books Australia Ltd, 487 Maroondah Highway, PO Box
257, Ringwood, Victoria 3134, Australia
Penguin Books Canada Ltd, 10 Alcorn Avenue, Toronto, Ontario,
Canada M4V 1E4
Penguin Books (NZ) Ltd, 182–190 Wairau Road, Auckland 10,
New Zealand

Typeset in Glasgow and Minion to an original design by
The Tipbook Company bv

Printed in The Netherlands by Hentenaar Boek bv, Nieuwegein

No part of this book may be reproduced in any form without
permission from the publisher except for the quotation of brief
passages in reviews.

The publishers and authors have done their best to ensure the
accuracy and currency of all the information in The Rough Guide,
however, they can accept no responsibility for any loss, injury or
inconvenience sustained as a result of information or advice
contained in the guide. Trademarks and/or usernames have been
used in this book solely to identify the products or instruments
discussed. Such use does not identify endorsement by or affiliation
with the trademark owner(s).

© The Tipbook Company bv, 2001

152 pp

A catalogue record for this book is available from the British
Library.
1-85828-654-9

THE ROUGH GUIDE TO
Flute and Piccolo

Written by

Hugo Pinksterboer

ROUGH GUIDES

THE ESSENTIAL TIPBOOK

Rough Guide Tipbook Credits

Journalist, writer and musician **Hugo Pinksterboer** has written hundreds of articles and reviews for international music magazines. He is the author of the reference work for cymbals (*The Cymbal Book*, Hal Leonard, US) and has written and developed a wide variety of musical manuals and courses.

Illustrator, designer and musician **Gijs Bierenbroodspot** has worked as an art director in advertising and for magazines. While searching in vain for information about saxophone mouthpieces, he came up with the idea for this series of books on music and musical instruments. Since then, he has created the layout and the illustrations for all of the books.

Acknowledgements

Concept, design and illustrations: Gijs Bierenbroodspot

Translation: MdJ Copy & Translation

Editor: Duncan Clark

KIRKLEES CULTURAL SERVICES	
250 480 202	
Askews	17-Mar-2003
788.32	£6.99
DE	CUL30851

IN BRIEF

Have you just started to play the flute? Are you thinking about buying a flute or a piccolo? Do you already have one and want to know more about it? Then this book will tell you all you need to know. You'll read about buying or renting a flute, about headjoints, closed hole and open hole keys and special mechanisms, about tuning and maintaining your instrument, about the flute's history and the members of the flute family. And much, much more.

Get the most from your flute

Once you've read this Rough Guide, you'll be in a position to make a good choice when you go to buy a new or used flute or piccolo, and to get the most out of your instrument. The book also explains all the flute-related jargon you're likely to come across in books, magazines, brochures and the Internet.

The first four chapters

If you've only just started playing, or haven't yet begun, pay special attention to the first four chapters. If you've been playing for longer, you may want to skip ahead to chapter 5.

Glossary

Most of the flute terms you'll come across in this book are briefly explained in the glossary at the end, which doubles as an index.

CONTENTS

1. THE FLUTE

The flute is a very popular instrument used in many styles of music, from classical to jazz, folk and rock. This chapter gives an overview of the flute and the people who play it.

If you want to play classical music, you can do so in all kinds of orchestras and groups – in a duo with another flute player or a pianist, for example, or as one of the two or three flute players in a symphony orchestra, along with fifty or more other musicians.

Flute ensembles
Flute ensembles, or *flute choirs*, only contain flutes. Like normal choirs, flute choirs generally focus on classical music but also perform arrangements of pieces in many other styles.

Wind ensembles
Wind orchestras, concert bands and show bands often include several flute players, as well as dozens of other wind players and a number of percussionists.

Military groups
The flute also features in various military groups such as fife and drum corps. Special *fifes* are still sometimes used, but more and more they're being replaced by the type of flutes you'll read about in this book.

Jazz, Latin and rock
The flute is becoming more and more common in jazz –

in standard modern jazz ensembles as well as fusion out-fits – and Latin music. You won't come across as many rock flute players, but there are some out there. Ian Anderson of the British band Jethro Tull, for example, made flute-rock famous more than thirty years ago.

Singing and growling

When you hear flutes used in non-classical styles, you may be surprised by the sounds they're capable of making. Adventurous players may 'sing' along while playing, growl through their instrument, or blow extra hard to create special tones and effects.

Orchestras and groups

You can read more about the differ-ences between all the orchestras, ensembles, choirs and other groups mentioned above in Chapter 12.

Buying and renting

Flutes are less expensive to buy than some instruments, and a decent one won't cost you the earth. However, they're not cheap, so you might want to consider renting one when you first start, to make sure it's the in-strument for you. You can read more about buying and renting flutes in Chapters 4 and 5.

No strings attached

As a flute player you have no strings, heads, reeds or batteries to replace. You just need your instrument, a cloth and a cleaning rod to dry it with after playing and a case or bag. And because it's such a small instru-ment, you can easily carry it around with you.

Just a few months

Another thing which makes the flute an attractive instrument to learn is

A piccolo and a flute

that with half an hour's practice every day, you should be able to play quite a lot in just a few months.

In tune

Although it's relatively easy to pick up the basics of flute playing, some things take much longer to learn, such as playing perfectly in tune. Just like a singer or violinist, a flute player has to carefully control the tuning – it's not like playing the piano, where the tuning is out of your hands.

Types of flute

There are many types of flute in the world – from bamboo instruments to keyless experimental models. This book deals primarily with the standard modern instrument, which is known by a number of names.

Transverse flute

The modern flute, like any flute which you play sideways – with the instrument horizontal – is a *transverse flute*. A few centuries ago, this term was essential to differentiate between the early version of today's flute and the recorder, which the term 'flute' originally referred to.

Boehm flute

Another name for the modern flute is the *Boehm flute*, after the German flute-maker Theobald Boehm, who built the first one in 1847.

Just flute

Other players call this instrument *C flute*, *concert flute*, *soprano flute* or even *standard flute*, but most simply call it 'flute'. If you see only this word after a name on a CD, you can be pretty sure the instrument being played is a Boehm flute.

Piccolo, alto flute and bass flute

The piccolo is a much smaller version of the flute, and as such it sounds a good deal higher. The *alto flute* and the *bass flute* are larger versions, so they sound lower. All these instruments are covered in this Rough Guide.

Flautists and flutists

Depending on the country you're in, a person who plays

the flute is called a *flautist* (UK) or *flutist* (US). As a flute player, you may also find yourself described as a *wind player*, because the flute, like all instruments that you blow into, is a *wind instrument*.

2. A QUICK TOUR

With all its keys, rods and levers, a flute looks more complicated than it really is. In this chapter you'll get to know what all the parts are called and what they do – the standard flute is dealt with first, and then the piccolo, alto flute and bass flute are discussed.

Basically, a flute is just a long tube with holes in it. You make the lowest tone by closing all of these *tone holes* – just like playing a recorder. If you open the last hole, the tone rises. If you also open the hole next to it, the tone rises some more. And so on.

Keys
On a flute, the tone holes are too large to close off, or *stop*, with your fingers as you would on a recorder. They are also too far apart. That's why a flute has *keys*. These keys and all the rods and springs that go with them are together called the *mechanism* or *key mechanism*.

Three parts
A flute usually consists of three parts. The first is the *headjoint* or *head*. This is the part with the *mouth hole* or *embouchure hole* – the hole you blow into. Then comes the long *middle joint* or *body*, with most of the keys on it. The bottom section – the *footjoint* or *foot* – usually has three keys for the lowest notes, which you operate with the little finger on your right hand.

The lip plate
Mounted on the headjoint is the *lip plate* or *embouchure*

crown

lip plate

mouth hole

headjoint

body

footjoint

A flute usually consists of three parts

plate, against which you place your lower lip. When you blow, you direct the air-stream against the *blowing edge* or *strike wall*: the opposite edge of the mouth hole. If you do it properly, you'll hear a tone – just like blowing across the top of a bottle.

The crown

One end of the headjoint is open; this bit slides inside the body. The other end, however, is closed off by a cap called the *crown*. What you can't see is the *stopper* or *tuning cork*, which is located inside the headjoint. To play in tune, the stopper must be in exactly the right place.

Pads

In order to close off the tone holes properly, the *pad cups* or *key cups* (the 'lids' of the keys) have soft *pads* inside them. These are discs of felt covered with a very thin membrane.

Tone holes

Most flutes have thirteen large and three small tone holes. The small ones are those closest to the headjoint.

Open and closed

Most tone holes are open when you're not playing, but with four of them it's the other way around: they are closed unless you press the keys connected to them. These special keys are called *touch pieces, key touches, touches, spatulas* or *levers*. You can see the G-sharp lever and the D-sharp lever on the illustration on page 10.

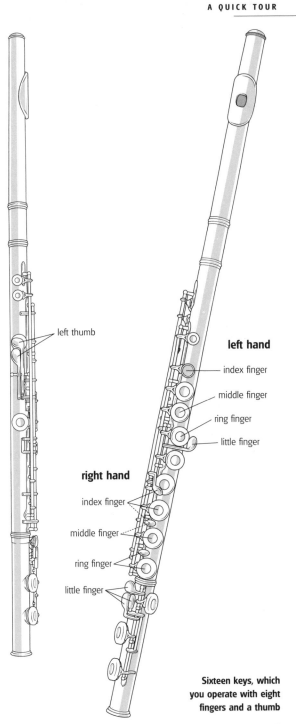

left thumb

left hand

index finger

middle finger

ring finger

little finger

right hand

index finger

middle finger

ring finger

little finger

**Sixteen keys, which
you operate with eight
fingers and a thumb**

Sixteen keys, nine fingers

Most flutes have sixteen keys, which you work with eight fingers and one thumb. How? First, you operate three, and sometimes even four, keys with your right-hand little finger alone. And often two keys close when you only press one down.

Trill keys

With your right hand you also operate a few special *trill keys*. When you press down the D-sharp trill lever, much further along, close to the headjoint, the small D-sharp trill key opens.

pad   pad cup

Pads make sure the keys stop the tone holes properly

Open hole flutes

On some flutes you may find that five of the key cups have holes in the middle. These are the keys on which your fingers rest (A, G, F, E and D), and you stop the holes with your fingertips. A flute with these holes is called an *open hole flute* or a *French system flute*; a flute without them is called a *closed hole flute* or *plateau flute*.

Beginners and open holes

Most professionals play open hole flutes, and in some countries, players are generally encouraged to start off on an open hole instrument. However, in other countries nearly all players start on a closed hole flute.

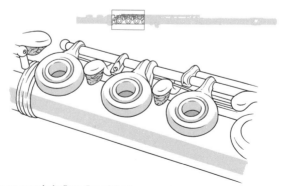

On an open hole flute, five of the keys are open

Springs

In order to make sure the keys open again after you press them down, a flute has a series of small springs resembling needles – which is why they're sometimes known as *needle springs*. You can see them if you look at the mechanism from the side, and they're also clearly visible on the illustration on page 42.

Cleaning rod

Every flute comes with a *cleaning rod*. After playing, you wind a cloth around it and clean the inside of the flute with it. The rod also serves to see if the stopper is in its proper position (see page 82).

Wooden and metal cleaning rods

Key names

The names of most of the keys and levers tell you which note you hear if you press down that key or lever. They're all shown on the illustration on the next page.

The C

With all the keys closed, you play the lowest note you can play on a flute. On the 'regular' C flute that note is the C. This is why the lowest key, right at the bottom of the foot, is called the C key. You close this key with the *C roller*.

The D

If all the keys up to and including the low D key are closed, you play a low D. In other words, a key is named after the note you hear when that key is the last one closed. If the E key, and all the keys up to it are closed, you'll hear an E. And so on.

The other way around

Some players use a different reasoning. They name each key after the note you hear when it is open. In this case, the D key, for example, becomes the E key: by opening this key you open the E tone hole and you hear an E.

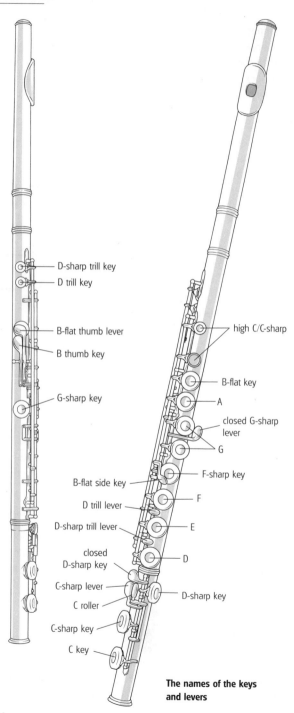

D-sharp trill key
D trill key

B-flat thumb lever
B thumb key

G-sharp key

high C/C-sharp

B-flat key

A

closed G-sharp lever

G

B-flat side key
D trill lever
D-sharp trill lever

F-sharp key

F

E

closed D-sharp key
C-sharp lever
C roller

D

D-sharp key

C-sharp key

C key

The names of the keys and levers

Fake key

The key for your left index finger, known as the *high C* or *C-sharp key*, is a 'fake key': there's no tone hole below it. The key operates the key cup a few centimetres up the tube.

In-line or offset

If you look at the flute on the opposite page you'll see that the two G keys (in the middle of the flute) are positioned slightly further outwards than the other keys, making them a little easier to reach. This design is known as an *offset G*. On other flutes you may see an *in-line G*, which means that those two keys are exactly in line with the others. The illustration on page 45 shows the difference very clearly.

Fingering charts

Fingering charts show you which keys to press to produce a particular note. The keys to be closed are shown in black, as you can see on the following diagram. Fingering charts are included in many teaching books.

A fingering chart showing the note G – if you press down the keys shown in black, you will play a G

Numbers

Some books use tables of numbers instead of fingering charts. The numbers refer to your fingers: 1 usually means your left index finger, 2 your left middle finger, and so on.

RANGE

If you only play the keys for your left hand shown in the fingering chart above, you'll hear a low G. But on a flute you can also play two higher-sounding Gs. You play these notes by blowing slightly differently – by *overblowing*. For some notes you have to use the same fingering when overblowing, for others you use a slightly different one.

Three octaves

On a flute you can not only play three different Gs, but also three As, three Bs, and so on. There are even a few notes you can play at four different pitches. The musical difference between two notes with the same name – such as one G and the next G – is an *octave*, so the flute can be described as having a range of just over three octaves. The following diagram shows the ranges of the flute, alto flute, bass flute and piccolo on the piano keyboard (eight white notes equals one octave).

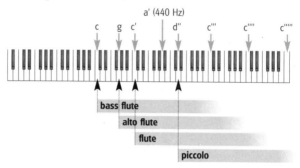

High and low
In the diagram above, the note names are written in various different ways – c, a', c''' and so on. This is a system of writing down note names that allows you to refer to a specific octave. A flute's low C can be described as c' (with a small letter c); this note is also described as *middle C*, because it's in the middle of the piano keyboard. The highest C you can play on a flute is c''''. You can read more about this and other systems of naming notes in *The Rough Guide to Reading Music and Basic Theory*. Also marked on the diagram is the tuning note A = 440 Hz. This is discussed on page 55.

The high E
Very competent players can go a few notes even higher than shown above, but these super-high notes are only used rarely. So when a player talks about a 'high E', they mean e''' and not e''''.

PICCOLOS
A piccolo is half the size of a flute, and this makes it sound exactly one octave higher, as you can see from the keyboard diagram above. The mechanism looks slightly different, but it works in exactly the same way.

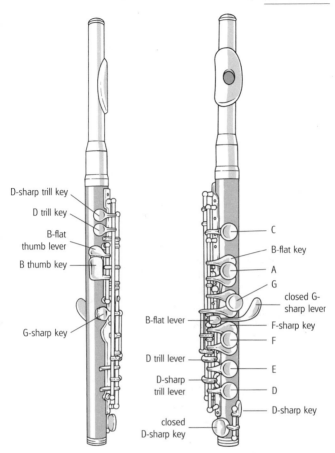

D-sharp trill key
D trill key
B-flat thumb lever
B thumb key
G-sharp key

C
B-flat key
A
G
closed G-sharp lever
B-flat lever
F-sharp key
F
D trill lever
E
D-sharp trill lever
D
D-sharp key
closed D-sharp key

A plastic piccolo with a metal headjoint. The names of the keys are the same as on a flute.

Wood, plastic and metal
The tube of a piccolo is often made of wood or plastic, but there are metal piccolos too.

Two parts
A piccolo consists of two parts: a headjoint and a body. Because there is no footjoint, the lowest note is a D, not a C (as the C key of a flute is on the footjoint).

The headjoint
All metal piccolos and some plastic piccolos have metal headjoints. Most wooden piccolos have one made of wood. A wooden headjoint has no lip plate.

Differences

The mechanism of a piccolo looks slightly different from that of the flute, because of the offset *touchpieces* above the double keys, such as the A. You play by putting your fingers on these touchpieces. Another difference is that there's one less key near the headjoint – the key missing is the 'fake key' for high C; on a piccolo, you operate the high C key directly, with your left index finger.

An octave higher

On paper, piccolo music looks just like flute music, but the notes sound an octave higher. If you were to write them down as high as they sound, most of the notes would end up far above the stave, which would make them harder to read.

ALTO FLUTES

An alto flute is quite a bit longer than a C flute, and as a result it sounds lower – four whole tones lower, to be precise. This difference in pitch is called a *fourth* or *perfect fourth*. It is equivalent to any gap of four white keys (except F–B) on a piano.

Offset touchpieces

Because an alto flute is bigger, the keys are further apart. To make sure you can still reach them all, some of the keys have offset touchpieces.

Curved headjoint

An alto flute is much longer than a normal flute, so you have to stretch your arms to play it – especially your right arm. This

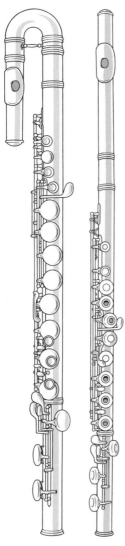

An alto flute with
a curved headjoint (left)
is no longer than
a C flute (right)

can make it a tiring instrument to play. Using a *curved headjoint* solves this problem, as it makes the alto flute the same length as a C flute. Curved headjoints are also found on other large flutes, such as the bass flute, and on some children's flutes (see page 19).

A C?

If you give a flute player an alto flute and ask them to play a C (or read a piece of music showing the note C), they will hold down the same combination of keys as they would to play a C on a standard flute. However, the alto flute sounds a fourth lower, so instead of a C the note produced will actually be a G.

All the notes

The same is true of all the notes played on an alto flute. Each note sounds four whole tones lower than the note being read and fingered: a D on paper results in an A, a B-flat is actually an F, and so on.

Why?

Why does the alto flute sound four whole tones lower than the music it's reading? The reason is simple – to make everything easier for the player. The alto flute sounds a fourth *lower*, so music written for it is written a fourth *higher*. This way the player can read and finger the notes just as they would if they were playing a standard flute, and the notes which come out will be the ones that the composer wanted (as long as you don't use a normal flute to play a piece written for an alto flute, or vice versa). Otherwise, players would have to learn two fingering systems: one for the C flute and another for the alto flute.

Transposing instruments

So, when playing an alto flute, the notes on the music refer to fingerings rather than actual pitches. This makes the alto flute a *transposing instrument* – and the music you read from is a *transposed part*.

A nice sound

Why bother making alto flutes if they cause all this confusion? The reason is that they make a nice, rich sound and they can play lower notes that a standard flute.

In G

Because you hear a G when you read and finger a C, the alto flute is described as being *in G* or *pitched in G*. Similarly, alto saxophones are pitched in E-flat (you play a C but you hear an E-flat), and most trumpets and clarinets are B-flat instruments (you play a C but you hear a B-flat).

Piccolos

As mentioned earlier, a piccolo sounds an octave higher than the notes indicated on paper. However, when you read and finger a G on a piccolo, the actual note, though a different octave, is still a G, so the piccolo is not considered to be a transposing instrument.

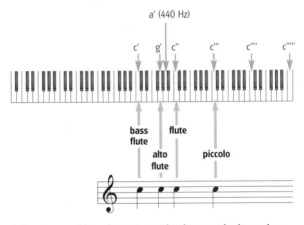

A C on paper and how that note sounds when you play it on a bass flute, an alto flute, a flute and a piccolo

BASS FLUTES

A piccolo is about half the size of a flute and it sounds an octave higher. The bass flute is twice the size of a flute, so it sounds an octave lower. You can see the tubes of these three instruments on the diagram on the opposite page.

Differences in design

Bass flutes always have curved headjoints; otherwise they would be far too long to play. All kinds of extra offset touchpieces and extended levers are also needed to operate the widely spaced keys. And because the instrument is heavier, there is a support, known as a *crutch*, to give

A piccolo is about half as big as a standard flute, and a bass flute is about twice as big

additional grip to the left hand. Sometimes this support is even used to attach the instrument to a floor stand, so the player doesn't have to support all the weight. The illustration on page 57 shows all these features. Bass flutes are very expensive, but there are budget versions available with PVC tubes (see page 107).

3. LEARNING TO PLAY

How hard is it to learn to play the flute? Do you need a teacher? Do you need to practise for hours every day? This chapter discusses these and other questions about learning the flute, and looks at special children's instruments.

The mechanism of a flute looks – and is – pretty complicated, but when you're playing you don't really notice it. All you need to know to play a wide variety of tunes are a few simple fingerings and how to blow properly.

Blowing

The first time you try to play the flute, you're likely to hear only the sound of rushing air. To make a note sound, you first need to learn how to blow properly. The better your blowing technique, the more tone and the less rushing air you'll hear.

Embouchure

How you blow also determines how well you play in tune and what type of tone you produce. For instance, if when you're blowing you increase the opening between your lips slightly, you'll immediately hear the sound change. The position of your lips and everything around them is called the *embouchure* – hence the alternative names for lip plate (*embouchure plate*) and mouth hole (*embouchure hole*).

A lot of air

Not all the air that a player blows goes into a flute. Every player also 'spills' a lot of air over the top – this is simply the way the instrument works. This doesn't mean you need to have huge lungs, but it does mean you need to learn how to properly control your breathing. You'll realize this the first time you play a few long notes on a flute; if you haven't learned proper breath control yet, you may well find yourself getting a bit dizzy.

Children's flutes

A normal flute is too long for many children younger than nine or ten to hold properly. That's why some manufacturers make special children's flutes, which usually have a curved headjoint to bring everything a bit closer to the player. However, not all teachers consider this a good solution, as a curved headjoint can lead to a bad posture. Flutes with curved headjoints are also harder to assemble, because you don't have much room to hold them without touching the keys.

No footjoint

There are also children's flutes with other adaptations. Some have no footjoint, for instance. This makes them shorter, and means the lowest note is a D. The two small trill keys, which you don't use to start with anyway, may also be omitted. Offset touchpieces may be added to some of the keys and the G-sharp lever may be extended to make it easier to reach. Some of these aids can also be added to normal flutes, as can special supports (see pages 64–65).

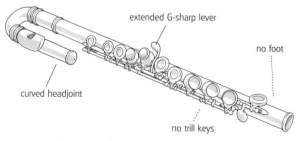

extended G-sharp lever

no foot

curved headjoint

no trill keys

A special children's flute (Jupiter)

Plastic flutes

Some children also start on a simple, plastic flute without keys. Plastic models are available for as little as £6/$10, but there are also higher-quality versions on the market.

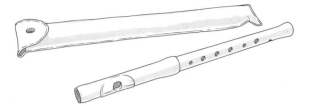

A plastic flute without keys (Yamaha)

Piccolos

Is a piccolo easier for children to play, because it's so small? Not really. Piccolos may be easier to hold than flutes, but they're also harder to learn to play. Also, piccolos and flutes are not quite as similar as many people think. Someone who plays the flute well won't necessarily be able to pick up a piccolo and play it well straightaway.

Playing with braces

If you have a brace on your upper teeth you will probably be able to continue playing, although it may take a while to get used to. And you'll have to readjust your playing every time the brace is adjusted. A brace on your lower teeth is trickier – after all, you place the flute against your lower lip when you play. Ask a flute teacher and your dentist for advice if you're getting a brace, or if you already have one and you want to start learning the flute.

Tingling

Some people with braces feel a slight tingling when they play the flute. This is caused by tiny electric currents generated by the combination of metals in your brace and flute. It's not dangerous, but it can be annoying.

Jaws and teeth

Playing the flute can be difficult or even impossible if your lower jaw sticks out much beyond your upper jaw or if you have a large overbite (if your upper jaw is very far forwards compared to your lower jaw). If this applies to you, ask a teacher for advice before you go to buy a flute.

LESSONS

You can find all the fingerings you need to play the flute in teaching books. But for a good embouchure, tone and technique, and for proper breath control, you can't really do without a teacher. A teacher will also help you learn a good posture, without which you may end up with pains in your shoulders or neck – either straightaway or after a few years.

Finding a teacher

Music stores often have private teachers on staff, or they can refer you to one. You could also ask your local Musician's Union, or a music teacher at a high school or music college in your area. Also check the classified ads in newspapers and music magazines and try the *Yellow Pages.*

Group and individual tuition

While most people take individual lessons, you could also opt for group tuition if it's available in your area. Personal tuition is more expensive – expect to pay around £15–30/ $20–50 per hour – but it can be tailored exactly to your needs.

Music schools

You may also want to check whether there are any music schools or teachers' collectives in your vicinity. These often offer good-value lessons (although in the UK they are not as subsidized as they used to be) as well as bonuses such as ensembles to play in and masterclasses.

Ask first

When enquiring about a music school or teacher, don't just find out how much lessons will cost. Here are a few other things you may want to ask:

- Is a **trial lesson included**? This will give you a chance to see if you get on with the teacher – and the flute.
- Is the teacher still interested in taking you on as a student if you are just doing it for **the fun of it**, or are you expected to practise for hours every day?
- Will you have to buy **a whole stack of books** or will the teaching materials be provided?
- Can the teacher **offer advice** on purchasing an instrument?
- Can you **record** the lessons, so that you can play them back at home?

Non-classical

Most flute players focus primarily on classical music, so most flute teachers tend to give 'classical' lessons. These can be a good place to start whatever you want to do with your instrument, but if you know you want to play non-classical music it's worth looking for a teacher who will be comfortable teaching the style you're interested in.

Listening and playing

One last tip: listen to the type of music you want to play as much as you can, and listen to other music too. Listen to CDs and to the radio, and better still, go to concerts. One of the best ways to learn to play is to watch other musicians at work. Top professionals or local amateurs, you can learn something from each one. And the very best way to learn how to play? Play a lot!

PRACTISING

There's no substitute for practice when you're learning to play an instrument. And the flute is no exception.

The lowest and the highest

On some instruments, such as the piano, it's just as easy to play the highest note as the lowest note. But on a flute the very lowest notes can be tricky, and it'll take you at least a year before you can play the very highest notes accurately.

Half an hour a day

With nearly all instruments it's better to practise half an hour every day than a whole day once a week. And this is especially the case with the flute – your breathing and embouchure will really benefit from daily practice.

Tone and tuning

Practice is also important for improving your tone and tuning. If you haven't been playing very long, soft notes will often sound too low (*flat*), while loud notes may sound a little too high (*sharp*). What's more, the low notes may sound too soft, while the high notes can easily be too loud. The more you play, the sooner you'll sort out those problems, and the sooner you'll learn to hear whether you are playing with good tuning.

The neighbours

You might not think it, but a flute can be nearly as loud as a piano or a trombone. If your neighbours or housemates are bothered by the sound of your playing, it may be enough just to agree fixed practice times. If you play a lot, though, it may be better to find somewhere else to practise, or even to soundproof a small room or part of a room. There's a variety of DIY-books on this subject, but you may be better off getting a professional to do the job.

On CD

Playing the flute is often more fun if you do it in a group. If there aren't any other musicians around, you could try one of the many CDs or CD-ROMs which provide music to play along to. Some contain the same piece of music three times: the first very slowly with piano and flute, so that you can play along to the flute part, the second time faster with only piano, and the third time in the correct tempo with a complete orchestra.

Computer lessons

You can also get special lessons on CD-ROM, with exercises, examples and music to play along to – some with entire orchestras.

Metronomes

All musicians should be able to keep steady time, not only drummers and conductors. For this reason, it's good to

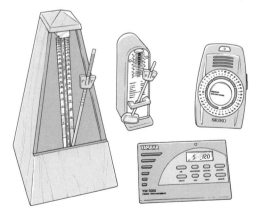

Two mechanical (clockwork) and two electronic metronomes

practise with a metronome – at least once in a while. This small device ticks or beeps out a steady adjustable pulse, helping you to work at tempo, timing and rhythm skills.

Recording

If you record your flute lessons, you can listen to what was said and played when you get home. Many musicians also record themselves practising every so often. This can help, because it's much easier to hear how you sound when you're not concentrating on playing. All you need is a hi-fi (or a personal stereo if you want to take it to your lessons), with a built-in or external microphone, although the better your equipment, the more enjoyable and instructive the recordings will be.

4. BUYING A FLUTE

This chapter deals with what you need to know before you go to choose an instrument, including how much you should expect to spend, the differences between budget and expensive models, and information about renting flutes and buying secondhand. The technical details that you need to look and listen for when you're testing and comparing instruments are dealt with in Chapter 5.

The cheapest new flutes cost around £300/$400, complete with case. Generally, the children's flutes mentioned in the previous chapter cost about the same. However, the most expensive flutes cost more than fifty times that much.

A little more money

Teachers often recommend that people start with an instrument a little more expensive than the cheapest ones – something in the region of £400–550/$500–$750. That extra money usually buys you a better-finished and more precisely built instrument. However, you won't necessarily be able to tell the difference unless you've been playing for a while, and until the instrument has been serviced (cleaned, oiled and adjusted) by a repairer.

More money, more silver

Most flutes costing up to around £600/$800 are silver plated. The more money you spend, the more solid silver is used – some instruments have a solid silver headjoint, others have the entire tube made of solid silver. Solid silver lasts longer and makes for a better sound.

Other differences

An expensive instrument shouldn't only be capable of producing a better tone than a cheaper instrument, it should also have a higher-quality mechanism that feels good to use and is less likely to need adjustment. More time and care will have been devoted to building the expensive instrument, and even smaller components may be made of better materials. What's more, you can order all kinds of extras, such as additional trill keys, or engravings on the keys and lip plate.

A pricey extra: an engraved lip plate

Professional instruments

Professional players often use instruments with mechanisms of solid silver. Such flutes are usually priced around £3000/$5000 or more, and are largely built by hand. Most conservatory students also play on handmade instruments, at least after their first year. It's possible to spend £20,000/$25,000 or more on a flute, though instruments this expensive are few and far between.

Someone who plays

You can read about how to spot the differences between one flute and another in Chapter 5. In order to hear those differences, you need to be able to play well – a problem if you're going to buy your first flute. So if possible make sure you take someone with you who can play, or at least go to a store where a member of the sales staff plays the flute.

SHOPS AND WORKSHOPS

The best place to buy a flute is a shop or workshop where flutes are also repaired and adjusted. Then you can be sure the staff know what they're talking about and you probably won't go home with a poorly adjusted instrument.

Checked and adjusted

The flute is a very precise instrument. All it takes is for one part to be bent minutely out of shape and you may not be able to play it properly. And if a pad doesn't close off a tone hole perfectly, you won't be able to play that note anymore – and probably a whole bunch of other notes, too. Whether they're expensive or cheap, even new flutes often need some extra adjustments before you can play them, which is why it's good to buy your instrument from somewhere that provides this service.

Overhaul

Just like a car, a flute needs to be checked and readjusted from time to time. If you buy a new instrument, this may be provided free of charge the first time it's needed, or for the first year, by the shop you bought it from. Some shops and technicians will send you a reminder when it's time for a service.

Renting

Flutes can also be rented. The rental period is often three months because that's usually enough to decide whether you want to carry on playing. It usually costs somewhere in the region of £25/$35 per month to rent a flute, though it can be much cheaper or more expensive depending on where you live and on the quality of the instrument. Usually the rent is based on a percentage of the price of the instrument – but the exact percentage varies from shop to shop.

Before you sign

If you want to buy the flute you've been renting, all or part of the rental fee you've paid so far may be deducted from the price if the shop has a 'rent-to-own' option. Ask about this before you rent in the first place. Also make sure you read your rental contract before you sign it, and check whether maintenance and insurance are included in the price.

Several shops

Many players will go to several shops or flute workshops before they buy. After all, different shops stock different brands, and different salespeople offer different advice.

Time and space

The more flutes there are to choose from in a shop, the harder the choice will be, but the better the chance of finding exactly the instrument you're looking for. Spend as long as you need comparing instruments, and don't rush into a decision. Some stores even have a separate room for testing instruments, so that you don't bother the other customers – and they don't bother you.

On approval

Some stores and workshops will give you one, two or more flutes on approval, so that you can assess them at home in your own time, though this option is mostly offered to experienced players choosing between high-quality instruments. As well as giving you lots of time to decide, this also has the advantage of letting you hear the instruments in the room you're used to practising in.

Every one's different

Even two 'identical' flutes, of the same make and model, will sound slightly different – regardless of the price range. So you should always buy the instrument you've tried out, and not the 'same instrument' from the storeroom.

SECONDHAND

Many flute players exchange their first instrument for a better one after a few years, and of course some people stop playing, so there are always plenty of secondhand flutes on sale.

A good deal

For as little as £200/$300 you can buy a carefully checked and properly adjusted secondhand flute that you'll be able to play for years. However, you can just as easily spend a fortune on a secondhand instrument. One of the advantages of a good secondhand flute is that you'll probably be able to sell it again later for a similar price, provided it's well maintained.

Private sales

Secondhand flutes can be purchased either at a music shop or from an individual – from an advert in a newspaper, bulletin board or Web site, for example. If you buy an instrument from an individual, you may well pay less than in a store. After all, the store owner needs to make some money on the sale too.

Shop sales
All the same, buying from a music shop or flute workshop does have some advantages. The instrument is likely to have been checked and regulated, and you'll usually get a warranty for six months, a year or even longer. You can usually choose between a number of instruments, and you can always go back if you have any questions. In some cases you can even exchange the flute you bought for a different one within a certain period. Also, a store owner will very rarely charge you much more than an instrument is worth – private sellers may, either because they don't know the real value, or because they think you don't.

A second opinion
If you plan to buy a secondhand flute – especially if you're checking out an instrument at someone's home – it's even more important to take someone with you who knows what they're talking about. Otherwise, you may turn down a valuable flute just because it's a bit dirty, or get saddled with an instrument that looks great but will actually never play well or sound good.

Appraisals
If you want to be really sure whether a used instrument is worth the money, get it appraised. Most stores can give you an appraisal, telling you what an instrument's worth, whether it needs any repairs and what they would cost. For more on buying secondhand instruments, see page 71.

Leaky flutes
Any decent flute can be made to sound good, even if it leaks like a sieve. But if you buy a leaking flute you should be aware that it may cost as much as £200/$300 to fix.

AND FINALLY
What you consider to be an ideal flute may well be the one used by your favourite player. But that doesn't mean

there's much point in trying to get the same type of instrument. Even if you can afford such a flute, you won't make the same sound – the tone depends more on the player than the instrument.

Brochures

If you want to know all about what's on sale, then go to a few stores and get hold of as many brochures as you can find. Don't forget the price lists to go with them.

Magazines, books and Web sites

If you want to read more, there are several magazines and other books that deal with flutes, and you can find loads of information on the Internet. For titles, Web addresses and other information see page 130.

Trade fairs

One last tip: if a music trade fair or convention is being held anywhere near you, go and check it out. You're likely to find a whole range of flute brands, not to mention dozens of players to provide information and inspiration. What's more, you'll be able to try out and compare whatever's on show.

5. A GOOD FLUTE

If you lay ten flutes side by side, it's hard to see any differences between them – they're all the same shape and size, and they have virtually the same keys in the same places. This chapter provides information on what to listen and look for when testing instruments, so you'll be able to spot the differences. Nearly all of these tips also apply to piccolos, alto flutes and bass flutes.

There are a few questions you'll always be asked when you go to choose a flute. Do you want a silver-plated flute or a solid silver model? That's what this chapter starts with. Would you prefer an in-line G or an offset G, open hole or closed hole keys, and do you want a split E mechanism? You can read more about these issues on pages 44–51. The headjoint, the most important component of a flute, is discussed from page 56 onwards.

With your ears

If you'd prefer to choose a flute just from how it sounds and feels, then go straight to the tips for play-testing and listening on pages 63–71. At the end of the chapter you'll find advice on buying secondhand flutes.

Different opinions

Whether they're talking about materials, mechanisms or manufacturers, flute players often disagree with each other about what's best. There are no right or wrong answers, and this chapter reflects both sides of some of the much-debated points. The only way to really find out what suits you best is by trying out as many instruments as you can.

MATERIALS

Flutes belong to the *woodwind* family of instruments. Today they're usually made of metal, but at one time they were all made of wood, and some players still opt for a wooden flute (see pages 36–37).

Silver plated

Nearly all inexpensive flutes are *silver plated*, the flute itself usually being made of nickel silver. Different manufacturers use slightly different types of nickel silver which vary in hardness – the harder the alloy used, the brighter the instrument may sound. Softer materials, such as brass, are slightly easier to damage and give a warmer sound.

Only the outside

Nickel silver sounds as though it ought to contain silver, but in fact it doesn't. The only silver in a silver-plated instrument is the ultra-thin layer on the outside.

Solid silver

Solid silver gives a richer, warmer, broader tone than silver plating. It can also allow you to 'colour' your tone more. The more money you spend on a flute , the more solid silver components you get – starting with the lip plate and the *chimney* (which connects the plate to the headjoint), then the whole headjoint, then the whole tube and finally the mechanism too.

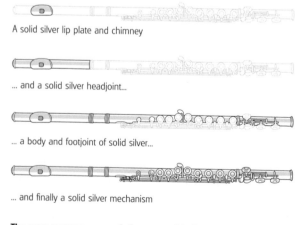

A solid silver lip plate and chimney

... and a solid silver headjoint...

... a body and footjoint of solid silver...

... and finally a solid silver mechanism

The more money you spend, the more solid silver you get

Silver lip plates and headjoints

The extra money you pay for solid silver is noticeable even if only the lip plate and chimney are made of this precious metal and the rest of the flute is silver plated. Though you can get a flute with a solid silver headjoint for around £600/$800, you can pay more for a higher-quality instrument which only has a solid silver lip plate and chimney.

Silver tube

The affect of a solid silver lip plate or headjoint is usually pretty obvious, but not many people will notice whether the body and footjoint are also made of solid silver. So why buy a flute with a solid silver tube? Because silver is more durable, because this type of flute is easier to repair, and because you can keep on polishing silver as often as you want. On a silver plated flute, the thin silver layer will wear through sooner or later. If you have very acid perspiration, even that may damage the silver plating. Solid silver will usually tarnish quickly if you don't look after it, but it hardly wears at all.

Silver mechanism

If you spend more than around £3500/$5000 on a flute, you may well get a solid silver mechanism. This will last longer and can easily be repaired if something gets bent or broken. Some players claim to be able to tell the difference in sound that a solid silver mechanism makes, but it's certainly an extremely minor difference.

Silver and silver

Another tiny difference that probably no one can really hear is that between flutes made of Britannia silver (958/1000 pure silver) and the more common sterling silver (925/1000). Sometimes the silver content is shown on the flute – you can tell from the number what type of silver you're looking at.

Always better?

Despite all the advantages of solid silver, some people still prefer to play a silver-plated instrument. Partly, this is because they tend to sound brighter or more open, and partly because you can buy a very well-made silver-plated instrument for the same price as an 'ordinary' solid silver flute.

Nickel and sores

Instead of silver, some flutes are finished with a layer of nickel. However, nickel can cause allergic reactions, including blisters and sores on the lips and skin, so it has been banned on new instruments in some countries. If you are very sensitive to nickel you might even have problems with a nickel silver flute. Some people use nail varnish or masking tape to protect their mouth (see page 95), but a preferable solution is to get a solid silver lip plate – or better still a solid silver headjoint.

Gold plating

If silver gives you a rash too, you can have your lip plate, headjoint or even your whole flute gold plated. This is also a solution if you have very acid perspiration, which can cause your flute to tarnish quickly or even go completely black. A tip: silver-plated flutes may be less sensitive than solid silver instruments in this respect.

The lip plate

Getting your lip plate gold plated will usually cost you around £50/$75. To gold plate a whole flute, the entire instrument has to be taken apart, and as a result the operation can easily cost £350/$500 or more. If you don't like the look of gold, you could have your lip plate or instrument finished with a silver-looking metal called rhodium instead. However, this is more expensive.

Advantages

One advantage of a gold plated flute is that it requires less polishing than a silver or silver-plated one. Also gold oxidizes less quickly than silver, so a gold-plated mechanism is less likely to stick than a silver one.

Gold chimney and lip plate

Most experts agree that gold plating does nothing for the sound. But making components of solid gold can make a difference. For instance, a gold chimney is said to make for a full and warm sound, particularly in the third octave. Gold lip plates don't affect the sound, but they do feel noticeably smoother than silver ones. Some players like this extra smoothness, though others find gold lip plates too slippery.

Gold flutes

For around £10,000/$15,000 or more you can buy a solid gold instrument. Gold flutes are often described as sounding darker, fuller, warmer, sweeter and a little less bright or brilliant than silver instruments, but there are gold flutes that actually have a brighter sound than silver models. Gold is a very dense metal, so a gold flute is appreciably heavier than a silver one.

Other flutes

Some manufacturers produce flutes made of other materials such as platinum or their own metal alloys. Others make tubes of two layers fused together – one gold and one silver, for example, to create a sound somewhere between those of the two metals.

Quality and sound

An important tip: the quality of a flute is more significant than the material it's made of. If a flute with a silver plated headjoint costs roughly the same as one with a silver headjoint, don't automatically choose the silver one just because solid silver is supposed to be better. Choose the flute that's easiest to play, that sounds best and has the best mechanism. Sometimes you have to choose between the one that sounds best and the one with the better craftsmanship, but never go for an instrument just because of the material it's made of.

Wall thickness

If you are buying quite an expensive flute you may be given a choice of *wall thickness*. An instrument with a thicker wall gives a slightly 'thicker', heavier, stronger and darker tone and sounds less forced at high volumes. A *thinwall* flute has a lighter tone and a quicker response, and the sound carries further.

How thick?

If you have a choice between different thicknesses, you'll usually see the figures 014, 016 and 018 quoted. These figures are thousandths of an inch; in metric terms this is 0.35, 0.41 and 0.46 millimetres. The harder the material is, the thinner the walls can be, though flutes with walls thinner than 014 are rare. Some flute-makers prefer to use

names to indicate thicknesses. This can be confusing – while one calls 014 'thin' another calls the same size 'very thin'.

Thin headjoints
Virtually all flutes have slightly thinner walls on the headjoint than on the body. If this is not the case, a flute will be very hard work to play – it will have a poor response. Flute players sometimes describe such an instrument as having a lot of 'resistance'.

Wider
Flutes are approximately 0.75" (around 19mm) wide on the inside. The wider the tube is – and hundredths of an inch count – the darker the flute may sound.

Bass flutes
The bass flute and other even lower-sounding flutes are becoming increasingly common in flute ensembles. As well as metal bass flutes, which often cost around £3500/$5000, there are much less expensive instruments made of PVC (see page 107).

WOODEN FLUTES
The wooden flute has recently made something of a comeback, and not only for historically accurate performances of music written before the metal flute was invented. More and more wooden flutes are found in classical orchestras and ensembles, used by players who prefer their warm, round, husky sound, which blends well with other instruments.

Increasingly popular again: the wooden flute

Grenadilla
Most wooden flutes are made of grenadilla, a very hard, almost black

wood. This wood, which is also known as African black-wood or M'Pingo, is also used for piccolos, clarinets and oboes. Softer varieties such as boxwood and cocuswood give a slightly softer, warmer, deeper tone.

Headjoint only

Instead of a flute made entirely of wood, some players opt for a metal instrument with a wooden headjoint, which will sound somewhere between a wooden and a metal instrument. Most wooden headjoints are handmade by specialized headjoint producers, and they often cost £750/ $1000 or more.

Prices

Only a few companies and flute-makers produce wooden flutes. Prices start at around £1500/$2500, but most instruments cost more.

Playing the flute in

If you have just bought a new wooden flute, you are often advised to play it in carefully. Play at most five minutes, twice a day for the first week, ten minutes the second week, and so on. This reduces the risk of cracks appearing on the instrument.

PICCOLOS

Piccolos are available in metal, wood and plastic. Wooden models usually have wooden headjoints, and the other types usually have metal ones. You do also see combination sets, though, such as a wooden piccolo that comes with both a metal and a wooden headjoint, allowing you to vary your tone depending on what you want to play. You can use the metal one to produce a bright sound that carries well and the wooden one when you need a warmer sound that blends more easily with other instruments.

Metal headjoints

Unlike those with metal headjoints, piccolos with wooden headjoints usually don't have a lip plate. For this reason piccolos with metal headjoints feel more like regular flutes, and they're preferred by many players who often have to change between a (metal) flute and a piccolo.

Three piccolos: one made of wood, one made of plastic with a metal headjoint and one entirely of metal

Metal and wood

What goes for metal flutes also goes for metal piccolos: the cheaper ones are silver plated and generally the more you spend, the more solid silver you'll get. However, because piccolos are so small, they naturally sound very bright, and many players feel that those made of metal sound too shrill. This is why wooden and plastic piccolos are so common.

Tuning

Metal piccolos are very sensitive to temperature changes.

This is especially problematic if you play outdoors, for instance in a drum and fife corps or another kind of wind band. If the temperature rises even a little, the tuning goes up; if it gets colder, the tuning goes down. The same thing happens with other instruments too, but not as easily as with the piccolo.

Plastic

Piccolos made of plastic look very similar to those made of wood. The sound is similar, too, although a wooden instrument will usually have a slightly warmer and richer tone. Plastic does have a few advantages, however: it barely needs any maintenance and you don't need to play the instrument in (see page 37). What's more, plastic does not suffer from cold or warm weather, humidity or dry air, all of which can cause cracks in a wooden instrument. Even so, wooden piccolos are often used by members of orchestras that play outdoors.

Cheaper

Plastic piccolos are a lot cheaper than wooden ones. You can buy a good one for about £400/$600 – about the same as the very cheapest wooden piccolo.

Wood-grained plastic

The difference between a plastic and a wooden piccolo is easy to see: plastic is shinier than wood, and it usually doesn't have a grain. However, plastic instruments with a *wood-grained composite* do have a grain-like pattern. You may also come across plastics with names like ABS and Resotone.

Cylindrical or conical

The body and footjoint of a flute are *cylindrical*: the tube is the same width all the way along. Wooden and plastic piccolos, though, are *conical*: the tube gets steadily narrower towards the end. Metal piccolos come with both types of tubes – some manufacturers make them cylindrical, others make them conical.

The difference

The sound of cylindrical metal piccolos often carries further and the higher notes are easier to play. On the other hand, this type of piccolo has a tendency to sound rather shrill and it can be harder to play in tune in the lowest octave. Metal piccolos with a conical profile are said to sound a little fuller and to blend better with other instruments as a result. Their *intonation* is also supposed to be better: it's easier to play them in tune.

Support

Because metal piccolos are so thin, they are difficult to hold on to. That's why they almost always have a small support for the left index finger.

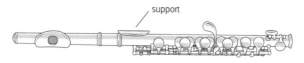

Support for the left index finger

THE MECHANISM

The mechanism of a flute consists of a series of keys and springs, plus a whole bunch of rods, corks and other small components. Alternative names for the key mechanism are *action*, *keywork* and *key system*.

Long key rods

A flute mechanism is easily damaged, and you need to take particular care not to knock or bend the keys and the long key rods. Several of these *key rods* contain other, thinner rods, which operate different keys. The long rod for the upper trill key (the D-sharp trill key), for instance, fits inside the rod for the lower trill key (the D trill key). If one rod takes a knock, you may find the other one stops working. Some other names for key rods are *rod-axles*, *axes* or *steels*.

Simultaneous closing

Many of the keys are coupled with other keys. For instance, if you press down the D or the E, the F-sharp key closes too. Of course, these coupled keys should always close simultaneously, not one slightly after the other. You can easily check for yourself. Try all the other keys and key combinations too.

Pad cups

The pad cups mustn't open too far or too little, they mustn't be sluggish or move too freely, and most importantly of all they must stop the tone holes completely. If they don't, you won't be able to play one or several notes properly, if at all. You can read how to test for a good seal on page 65.

With screws

Most instruments have a number of small screws that are used to make precise adjustments to the keys. Sometimes these adjustment screws are easy to see, but often they are hidden. Whatever type of screws they are, it's usually best not to meddle with them – adjusting is best left to a flute repairer.

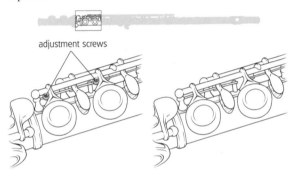

adjustment screws

On the left flute you can see the adjustment screws, but on the right flute they are hidden

Without screws

Expensive flutes often have no adjustment screws at all, and some manufacturers even offer a choice between flutes with or without them. A mechanism without screws will usually need adjusting less often, but when it does it takes more work. Some players like to have adjustment screws so that if something goes wrong when they're travelling or when there's no repairer nearby, they can always have a go at fixing the problem themselves.

With shoulders

If you read flute brochures and ads, you'll see that manufacturers use all kinds of screws, from 'tapered pivot screws with shoulders' to 'screws with nylon inserts'. The type of screws used doesn't really affect the player.

Springs

Brochures for expensive flutes also often tell you what material the springs are made of. One brand may use stainless steel – claiming that it stays at the proper tension and allows for the most precise adjustment – whilst another may use gold, saying it feels smoother and breaks less easily. Cheap flutes usually have springs made of phosphor bronze. Again, such fine technical details are not important compared to how an instrument sounds and plays.

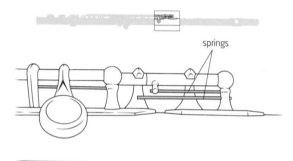

springs

Springs that look like needles

Bumpers

In a few places, such as under the D-sharp lever and under the trill levers, there are small bumpers to stop you pressing the levers too far down. Cork bumpers are usually a little quieter than bumpers made of neoprene, but they don't last as long and cost a bit more.

With or without pins

If you look at the long key rods on most flutes, you'll usually see a number of small, black pins, although there are a few brands that build *pinless mechanisms*. These have certain advantages: your clothes and fingers won't get caught on them; the oil inside them carries on doing its job better because there are fewer holes in the rods; and it's harder for perspiration and other moisture to get in. What's more, the manufacturers claim that certain keys, such as the B-flat, are less likely to stick if you have this type of mechanism. You can read about a fourth advantage on page 47.

Ribless piccolos

The rods of the mechanisms are attached to *pillars* or *posts*, which are virtually always soldered to two, three or more metal strips, called *ribs* or *straps*. In the past, posts were sometimes soldered directly onto the flute, without ribs. These days the only 'ribless' instruments you're likely to come across are certain inexpensive metal piccolos. Not having ribs saves a bit of time during manufacture, but it also makes the instrument a bit more fragile.

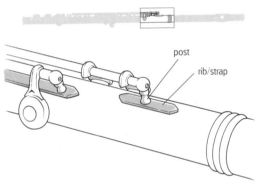

Posts and ribs

PADS

The pads of a flute must seal the tone holes perfectly. Just one leaking pad may be enough to stop you playing a whole series of notes.

Felt and membrane

Most pads consist of a layer of cardboard and a thin disc of felt covered by two ultra-thin layers of membrane. This membrane is sometimes called *bladder* or *fish skin* (or, in German, *Fisch Haut*), but it actually comes from cow intestines. This extremely thin material, also known as *goldbeater's skin*, tears very easily.

White, yellow and grey

These days, most flutes have yellow pads, but they may also be white or a dull grey colour. The grey ones are unbleached. According to most manufacturers, the only difference between yellow, white and unbleached pads is the colour. But there are differences in quality between various pads – handmade flutes usually have high-quality handmade ones.

Changing pads

Pads sometimes need to be changed, for instance because the membrane tears or becomes worn, or because the felt has become too thin. Moreover, felt is quite sensitive to moist or dry air.

Plastic

Manufacturers are always looking to develop pads which are more durable and don't expand or shrink. For instance, some pads use plastic instead of felt. Plastic pads are so flat that they only work on expensive, perfectly adjusted flutes with very precisely manufactured tone holes. Straubinger is one of the better-known makers of such pads.

Cork

Piccolos sometimes have a few pads made of cork or another material. If so, you're likely to find them on the keys in the 'spit track', such as the G-sharp and the D-sharp. Because they are lower down, these keys are more affected by the moisture in your breath as it collects inside the instrument. Cork pads are less sensitive to moisture, but they are a bit noisier.

MAIN CHOICES

When you're buying a flute you can often choose between closed hole or open hole keys, an in-line G or an offset G, and a model with or without a split E mechanism. These options, and the B foot, are explained over the following pages.

Your teacher

Many people who have only just started playing leave these choices to their teachers. In some countries, most teachers will start a pupil off on a flute with closed hole keys, an offset G and a split E mechanism, because it's easier to play. In other countries it's the other way round – teachers think it's better to start on a flute with open hole keys, an in-line G and no split E mechanism.

IN-LINE OR OFFSET G

Many years ago, Theobald Boehm realized that if the G keys are 'offset' slightly, moved closer to the left ring finger, they are just a little easier to reach. Even so, there are still many flutes without this type of mechanism – with an in-line G instead.

In-line

If the G keys are in line with the other keys, you need to stretch your left ring finger just a little further – especially if you have a flute with open hole keys, as this type of flute requires you to place your finger right in the middle of the key. With closed hole keys you can 'cheat' a little bit by putting your finger on the edge of the key.

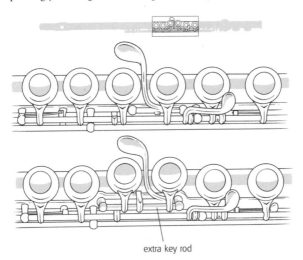

extra key rod

A flute with an in-line G (above) and one with an offset G. The offset G requires an extra rod.

No difference

Whether the keys are in-line or offset makes no difference to the sound. So why are so many flutes still sold with in-line Gs? The main reason is that some players think they look more attractive, and because it's a design which has been handed down from famous old French flute-makers. Some modern factories still make their flutes according to that old French tradition: all their flutes have open keys and in-line Gs. So if you want an offset G, you'll have to try a different brand.

SPLIT E MECHANISMS

On a flute without a split E mechanism, the high E (e''') is a difficult note to play. A split E mechanism makes this note a lot easier to reach: it speaks more easily and you're less likely to 'slip off' or 'split' it.

Closing the second G

You can recognize a split E by the small extra arm between the second G key and the F-sharp key. This arm closes the second G key when you play a high E, which makes that note speak more easily.

Not closing the second G

If you play a high E on a flute without a split E mechanism, the second G key simply stays open.

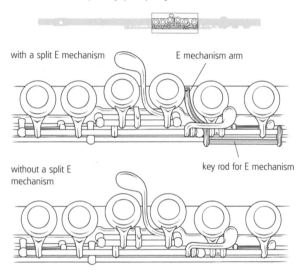

A split E is immediately recognizable by the extra rod and the small lever between the lower G and the F-sharp key

A little more money

Many experts say the only reason to buy a flute without a split E is to save a little money. On most low-budget flutes, the price difference is less than £30/$50 – sometimes you don't have to pay anything extra at all – but on professional models the difference may be £500/$750, or even more.

With or without

Some players prefer to play without a split E, because they think the extra closed key makes the high E a little duller, or because they think the split E is very delicate and doesn't always operate properly. Still, most players, including professionals, do use a split E.

On and off

There are various fingerings for almost all the notes you can play on a flute, up to eight or more for some. These alternate fingerings are often used to make certain notes easier to play loudly, or softly, or to make it easier to go from one note to another. If you have a split E, some of those alternate fingerings don't work, which is why some expensive flutes have a *clutch* with which you can disengage the split E mechanism.

Harder to repair

A number of brands don't fit split E mechanisms to their flutes with in-line Gs, because they say it makes them more difficult to make and to repair. This doesn't apply to flutes with pinless mechanisms.

Above or below

With an *under-key split E*, part of the E mechanism passes under the other keys. This is more expensive but less vulnerable to damage than the more usual *over-key split E*, and it looks a bit tidier.

Donuts

Instead of using an E mechanism, the high E can also be made easier to reach by setting a ring inside the second G hole. This ring or *donut* makes the hole just a bit smaller. Almost every brand of flute has its own name for these rings, from 'E disk' to 'NEL' to 'high E facilitator' to 'low G insert'.

Other effects

A donut also makes the high G-sharp and the high A easier to play. On the other hand, some say it makes the lower A notes sound a little too low because it half closes the G hole – but then again, you can adjust those notes with your embouchure.

Fitting a split E

If you have a flute without a split E, you can usually have one fitted. Before you do so, though, consider whether it would be better to exchange your flute for one which already has a split E. Also consider getting a donut fitted – this is a lot cheaper, with prices starting at about £30/$50.

Piccolos and alto flutes

Most piccolos are also available in two versions, with or without a split E. Alto flutes with split E mechanisms are less common, but they do exist.

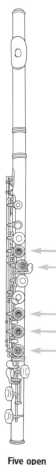

Five open hole keys

OPEN OR CLOSED HOLE KEYS

The five keys on which you place your fingertips can be either open or closed hole keys. Few people can hear the difference, but the sound isn't the only issue in choosing between them.

In the middle

It's easier to learn to play with closed hole or plateau keys, if only because you don't always have to put your fingers exactly in the middle of the keys. If you play with open hole keys and you don't put a finger in the middle of a key, air will escape. So a flute with open holes (a French system flute) forces you to put your finger in the 'proper' position, resulting in what is considered to be a correct posture.

Injuries

With open hole keys, your fingers (particularly your left ring finger) need to stretch a long way, especially if you have quite small hands and your flute doesn't have an offset G. This can result in nerve and muscle injuries.

Why open?

Closed hole keys are easier to play, they are sturdier, the pads are easier to replace, and a closed-key flute is easier to keep clean. So why would you opt for open hole keys?

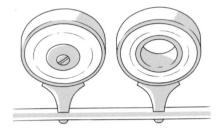

A closed hole key and an open hole key

Traditional designs
Most professional flute players use an instrument with open hole keys. Some think they sound better, some think they look more attractive, and others simply use them because the best quality flutes have them, which in turn has a lot to do with flute-making traditions.

Glissandos and multiphonics
On an open hole flute it's easier to play glissandos – sliding seamlessly from note to note. And open hole keys allow you to play extra *multiphonics* (two or more notes at once) and quarter tones (notes between two semitones, between C and C-sharp, for example). However, you only really need to use multiphonics and quarter tones if you play contemporary classical or avant-garde music.

Easier still
On the subject of quarter tones, multiphonics and glissandos: they are even easier to play on a flute with the *key- on-key mechanism* devised by Dutch flute-maker Eva Kingma. You play this type of flute in the same way as you would an ordinary flute, but there are six extra keys which give you all kinds of extra options.

Softer, richer, fuller?
Is there also a difference in sound between open hole and closed hole flutes? Some players think open hole instruments sound fuller and richer. Others think their tone is more even, or has more of a singing quality. But not everybody agrees on any of these points.

49

Feeling the keys

Just from listening, you probably wouldn't hear a difference between an open hole and a closed hole flute. Players sometimes say that they hear a difference when they are playing, but of course they can also feel the difference – and what you feel is all too easy to hear as well. Some people prefer open hole flutes purely for the feel.

Plugs

If you have bought or plan to buy an open hole flute, but cannot reach all the open keys properly, there are special *plugs* to close up the problem keys. These plugs can be inserted temporarily, if your hands still need to grow, or permanently, if you have fully grown but small hands. Most players only plug the keys they can't reach easily: usually the two keys which are operated with the ring fingers. There are cork plugs, transparent plugs which you can barely see, and silver plugs which make an open hole key look like a closed hole key.

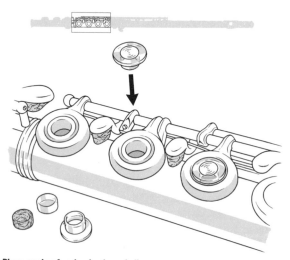

Plugs made of cork, plastic and silver

More money

Some makes have similar prices for open hole and closed hole flutes of the same series, others charge a little extra for an open hole model, and some charge quite a lot more – up to around £100/$150. A number of brands do not make open hole flutes in the lower price ranges.

Other names
Open hole keys are also known as *open hole cups, perforated keys, ring keys* or *open-ring keys*, and *French* or *French-style keys*. And a flute with such keys is a 'French model' flute. Alternative names for closed hole or plateau keys include *solid cups, covered keys* and *closed-ring keys.*

Cast or forged
One other technical detail about keys is whether they've been *forged* or *cast* (*die-cast*) into shape. Some claim that forged keys are better, though many expensive flutes have die-cast keys and many cheaper ones have forged keys. All in all, this isn't a particularly important consideration.

B FOOT
A *B foot* or *low B foot* is slightly longer than the regular *C foot* that is found on most flutes. This extra length allows you to go a semitone lower: to a low B, as the name suggests. This low B isn't used very often: if you play classical music, you won't come across it until you've been playing for a number of years, and it's used just as rarely in other styles. So don't worry about a B foot when buying your first flute.

Longer and heavier
A flute with a B foot is a good inch and a half (nearly 4cm) longer than an ordinary flute. This may not sound like a lot, but it makes an instrument feel substantially heavier.

A fuller sound
The extra length also changes the sound of a flute slightly. Fuller, warmer, richer, darker, bigger and deeper are the words often used to describe the resulting tone. A B foot is also said to improve the tuning of the highest octave.

A lighter sound
Despite the extra note and richer sound provided by a B foot, some players prefer to use a C foot. It is often said that a B foot makes the third octave a little harder to play, and that it causes the lowest notes to sound too low. But some players simply prefer the clearer, lighter sound of a C foot.

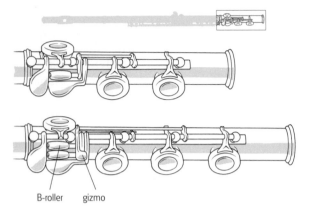

B-roller   gizmo

A B foot is longer and heavier than the normal C foot

Gizmo

There's one thing everyone agrees on: a B foot makes the highest C (c'''') a little dull. That's why just about every B foot has an extra lever which closes the B key when you play that note, making it sound brighter. This little mechanism is known as the *gizmo*.

Prices

How much extra you pay for a B foot depends on the brand and the price range you're looking at. A B foot for an inexpensive flute usually costs around £100/$150 extra; on a high-budget flute the difference is often £750/$1000 or more.

Other feet

There are various less common varieties of foot, including the B foot with detachable B-section, the short D-foot and the B foot for alto flutes.

EXPENSIVE FLUTES

Some features are found only on expensive flutes. Pointed pad cup arms or soldered tone holes, for instance, or special trill keys, or flutes in several keys.

Pointed cup arms

Expensive flutes can often be recognized by their *French-style cup arms*, which end in a sharp point in the middle of the cup – hence their other name, *pointed cup arms*.

Y- or C-style arms

Cheaper flutes have arms which partly follow the curve of the pad cup. They are usually called *Y-* or *C-arms*, because they are shaped a little like these letters. However, even the most

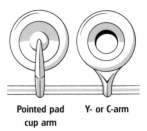

Pointed pad cup arm   **Y- or C-arm**

expensive flutes always have the Y-style arms for the open hole keys, as this is the only type of arm you can fit to an open hole pad cup.

Extruded or soldered

Most flutes have *extruded* or *drawn* tone holes, which are made by drawing them out of the flute wall. The edges of these holes are very thin, so thin in fact that they would cut through the membrane of the pads if they weren't 'rolled' or 'folded'. *Soldered tone holes* are made differently – instead of being drawn and rolled, they have small metal rings soldered onto the tube.

Heavier

Soldering rings onto a flute makes it heavier, which some believe provides a darker, deeper or heavier tone. It also increases the flute's resistance – just like having a thicker wall.

A better seal

The edges of soldered tone holes are usually flatter and thinner than the edges of drawn tone holes. This helps to create a better seal when the instrument is properly adjusted.

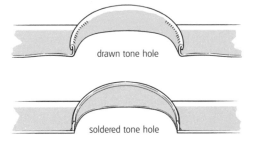

drawn tone hole

soldered tone hole

You can recognize a drawn tone hole by its rolled top. The bottom edge where the hole meets the tube is also more rounded that on a soldered tone hole.

The only possible drawback, apart from the additional weight, is that the rings may leak where they meet the tube, but this is very rare.

Extra rollers

A little roller can make it easier to move your little finger from the C-sharp lever to the D-sharp lever. Some flutes have one roller (either for the C-sharp lever or for the D-sharp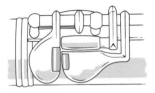

C-sharp and D-sharp rollers

lever), some have two (one on each lever) and many flutes have none.

G/A trill key

The high G/A trill is hard to play, which is why some flutes have a special G/A trill mechanism, which consists of two keys (one to the left of the thumb keys and one to the right) which are operated with a single lever.

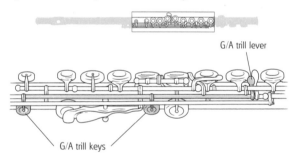

G/A trill lever

G/A trill keys

G/A trill keys and lever

C-sharp trill

You can also make the high G/A trill easier to play by paying an extra £350/$500 or more for a flute with a C-sharp trill key. This extra key is intended especially for trills from C and B to C-sharp, but it also makes the G/A trill and more than ten other trills easier. And it also allows you to play the high G-sharp very softly, yet in tune.

Other special features

There are many more special keys you can have fitted to your flute. The *Brossa F-sharp*, for example, designed for

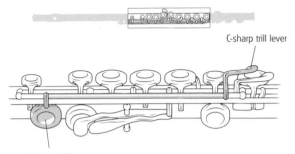

C-sharp trill lever

C-sharp trill key

You operate the C-sharp trill key with your right index finger

certain trills with that note, or a separate B/C trill key, or
an *open G-sharp*. With an open G-sharp, the G-sharp key
on the bottom of the flute disappears; the lever by your left
little finger which is commonly used to open this key now
closes the second G key. When playing high E you close
this key too, which means a split E is not necessary. Flutes
with an open G-sharp often have *reverse B/B-flat thumb
keys*, meaning that the keys operated by your left thumb
work the other way round.

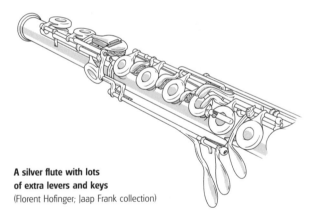

**A silver flute with lots
of extra levers and keys**
(Florent Hofinger; Jaap Frank collection)

Tunings

The A slightly to the right of the centre of a piano keyboard
(see page 12) is often used as a tuning note. The note is
described as the 440 hertz A, as it is caused by 440 vibrations per second. Most flutes, like most other instruments,
are built to play an A at 440 hertz when they're properly
tuned.

A little higher

In Europe, some orchestras and ensembles tune to a slightly higher pitch, and if you want to play in such a group your instrument should ideally be built to play at whatever pitch is used. This is why some brands and makers offer flutes in 442, 444 or even 446 hertz, though usually only in the more expensive models.

THE HEADJOINT

The sound of a flute is mostly formed in the headjoint. If you put a different headjoint on a flute, it sounds like a different instrument. This explains why there's a wide variety of headjoints available, with prices to meet all budgets.

A better sound

Are you fed up with the sound of your cheap flute but unable to afford a better one? If you fit your instrument with a good solid silver headjoint you'll probably notice a big improvement. A flute that cost around £400–550/$600–750 may well be worth fitting with a silver headjoint of a similar price – some stores even offer such combinations new. Before rushing out to buy a new headjoint for your flute, though, consider having your instrument valued to see if it's worth the investment.

A different sound

Many flute players with expensive instruments also experiment with and switch between different headjoints – not just to improve the sound, but to get a wide range of timbres. One headjoint can provide a warm, deep tone, and another a bright sound which projects well.

Choosing

In general, you'll only be offered a choice of headjoints if you are buying an instrument in a high price range or from an expensive brand. Some brands, though, do offer a choice with lower-priced flutes. Not every headjoint fits every flute, although they can almost always be made to fit.

Different players

How a headjoint makes a flute sound depends on many different things, including the player: a headjoint that

support
or crutch

An alto flute with a curved headjoint, one with a straight headjoint and a bass flute

makes one person sound great may not work for someone else.

The naked eye

The material of the headjoint contributes greatly to the sound (see page 32), but so do the shape of the mouth hole and the lip plate, and many other factors. Many of the differences are so small that they can't really be seen with the naked eye but you will hear and feel them when you play.

Advice

If you know roughly what type of sound you want to achieve, a good salesperson will be able to pick out the possible options, so you won't have to try out fifty different headjoints. If you've got a lot of money to spend and you know exactly what you want, you could even go and talk to a headjoint maker and have a headjoint crafted to your exact requirements.

Curved headjoints

As was noted in Chapter 3, children's flutes are the only C flutes you're likely to come across with curved headjoints. On alto flutes, though, they're very common, because a straight headjoint makes the instrument so long. Though it can be tiring on the arms, some players opt for a straight alto flute because they don't like the balance of a curved instrument.

A different sound?

Opinions vary about how a curved headjoint affects the sound of a flute. They are often said to produce a mellower, more rounded tone, but some players find they provide poorer response and intonation.

Different models

Without a curved headjoint, a bass flute would be far too long – the player simply wouldn't be able to reach all the keys. Apart from the regular U-shaped headjoint, you may also come across bass flute headjoints in various other shapes. Unusually shaped headjoints are also sometimes used on other types of flutes, most commonly to prevent or relieve shoulder and neck problems.

HEADJOINT MEASUREMENTS

Most brands make various different headjoints: one for a bright sound and another for a dark sound, one for a very focused tone with great projection, and another for a sweet, light timbre. If you were to lay all these headjoints side by side, the differences would probably be barely visible, if at all, because the physical differences are very small.

No two are the same

Because the very smallest differences between two head-joints can make a different sound, no two sound identical. This is the main reason why no two flutes – even if they're the same model from the same brand – ever sound exactly the same.

Tapered

Headjoints are about 0.08" (2mm) narrower at the crown than they are at the open end, and in between there is a very slight curve. The curve is so slight, that it cannot usually be seen by the naked eye. The exact shape of the headjoint as it narrows, which is described as the *taper*, is important to the sound. Some brands advertise headjoints with a *French taper*, supposedly offering a slightly more elegant and refined tone, or a *German taper*, with a richer, more solid tone.

Lip plate

The shape of the lip plate affects a flute's ease of playing and also its sound. Seen from the side, some lip plates are a little more rounded than others. If you look from above, you'll see that the hollow for your lower lip can also vary quite a bit. You will only discover what feels best or plays most easily by trying out all the different headjoints on offer. If you find it hard to appreciate the feel (and sound) of various types, you could start by trying two extremely different models.

Wings

A lip plate or wooden headjoint with a *winged embouchure* has 'wings' on either side of the mouth hole, and some lip plates look like they have a kind of wave in them. Both designs are meant to help direct your airstream, making it easier to play certain notes (low ones in particular) and to switch quickly between the high and low registers. However, it's often said that winged embouchures don't allow you to colour the sound as well. The bigger the wings are, the more marked their effect.

Who for?

Winged lip plates are good for people who don't play the flute very often and those who don't have a very well-developed embouchure. A winged embouchure can also benefit so-called *doublers* – people who play another wind instrument as well as the flute – as it makes it easier to switch from one instrument to another.

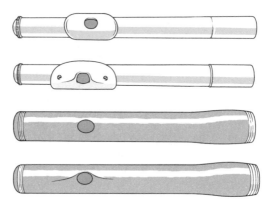

Metal and wooden headjoints with and without wings

Very small, very big

Some expensive lip plates have very small wings, supposedly enhancing the carrying power of the instrument and giving the player more room to colour the tone, as well as increasing the instrument's dynamic range. So-called *reform lip plates* are usually made of plastic and have large wings.

Mouth hole

Mouth holes vary in both shape and size. Most cheaper flutes have fairly large, almost rectangular mouth holes, which make it easy to produce plenty of volume. However, compared to a smaller or more oval mouth hole, the sound will be a little less refined and it won't be quite as easy to colour the tone. A smaller mouth hole makes playing harder, but it does give you more control and enables a better tone.

Overcut and undercut
On many flutes you will notice that the left and right edges of the mouth hole are slightly slanted. This is called an *overcut* mouth hole. A chimney or riser which is slanted at the bottom is *undercut*. How much metal has been cut away, how slanted the edge is and how concave or convex the edge is are all factors which influence the way a flute sounds and plays.

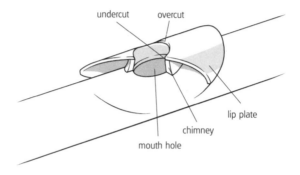

Mouth holes, lip plates and chimneys: no two are the same, but the differences are barely visible

Chimney
When it comes to chimneys, minute measurements can greatly affect the sound and feel of the instrument – mere hundredths or even thousandths of an inch can make a big difference. A high chimney or *riser* is said to give a bigger, darker sound, and the shape of the back wall also has an influence: the flatter that wall is, the louder and 'rougher' the tone supposedly becomes.

Visible differences
Some differences between two headjoints are easy to spot. For example, an overcut mouth hole is visibly different to one which isn't overcut. But this doesn't mean you can tell how a headjoint will sound by looking at it – there are many visible and invisible factors that combine to determine the sound.

A tube in a tube in a tube

When putting a metal flute together you slide the head-joint into the upper part of the body. Most wooden flutes and piccolos fit together in a different way. At the end of the wooden body is a small metal tube with a cork ring. This piece of tubing goes inside the headjoint. If you look inside the open end of the headjoint, you'll see a second piece of tubing. This piece fits inside the body.

Bubble, European and American

Having a double tube means you need extra space, which is why the headjoint is quite a lot fatter at the joint. Names for this kind of headjoint include *bubble style*, *bulb style* and *European*. Another type of headjoint for wooden piccolos has a metal tube which slides inside the body, just like a metal flute. This *American* system is commonly found on cheaper piccolos.

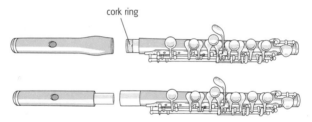

cork ring

A European-style piccolo with a bulge in the headjoint and an American- style instrument, both made by the same company (Emerson)

CROWN AND STOPPER

The crown closes off the headjoint at the top end and also helps keep the stopper in the correct position (see pages 81–83).

Plates

The traditional stopper or tuning cork looks like a small wine bottle cork with a thin metal washer at either end. In some cases the right-hand washer is concave rather than flat; this is said to make the tone a little warmer.

O-ring

Because cork doesn't last for years, non-cork stoppers are

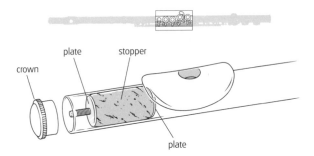

crown
plate
stopper
plate

becoming increasingly common. A stopper may be a plastic disc surrounded by a rubber O-ring, or a rubber ring jammed between two washers – the material has no noticeable influence on the sound.

Crown

The crown can affect the flute's sound. A heavier crown, for instance, can make the tone a little 'heavier', bigger or darker. Some experts think that gold is the best material for adding weight, but others say lead is just as good, claiming the weight is the only significant factor. If you really want to splash out, you can buy a gold crown set with an inlaid diamond for the price of a good student flute.

PLAYING

In the end, there's only one way to find out which flute, or which headjoint, is the right one for you: by playing lots of different models. When you try out a flute you'll discover how it behaves and how easily it plays, whether it seals properly and how it sounds.

The feel

One flute may feel more comfortable than another – because of the shape of the pad cups which your fingers rest on, for instance, or the positioning of the G keys, the length of the G-sharp lever or the transition between the little-finger levers and rollers. Small differences can count, too. For example, on most flutes, the C roller is just a little fatter in the middle than at the ends (*a tapered roller*) but some rollers are the same thickness all the way along, making them feel slightly different.

The mechanism

The best way to check whether the mechanism works properly is to 'play' the instrument without blowing. Listen for rattles when you press down and let go all the levers and keys, and check whether all the coupled keys respond immediately (see page 40).

Extensions

If there are certain keys or levers that you can't reach easily, you can have touch plates or extensions fitted, or you can fit them yourself. They are available in standard shapes and sizes but you can also have them made to your exact requirements.

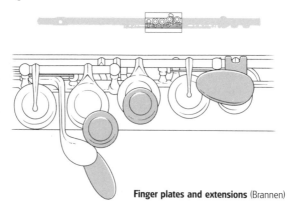

Finger plates and extensions (Brannen)

Rests

There are also all kinds of rests designed to improve your grip on the instrument. For example, the Bo-Pep brand offers rests for your right thumb and left index finger. You

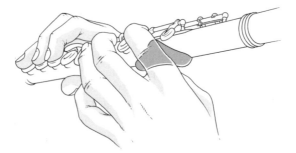

Rest for left index finger (Bo-Pep)

simply click them onto your flute, and they are just as easy to remove. Some players make their own rests from foam plastic insulation tubing (cut open one end and slide it onto the flute), Velcro or cork, which you can sandpaper to exactly the shape you want (or get someone to do it for you).

Seal

You'll only be able to hear what a flute can do if it seals properly: it must not have any leaking pads. You can check by playing every note from high to low, as softly as you can and with as little pressure on the keys and levers as possible. If you need to press hard to play a note, something is wrong. Another test is to go from a low G to a low C in one go, blowing very softly (close the C key whilst you are still playing the G). The C should come out straightaway.

Poppoppoppop

If you press down the keys and levers one by one without blowing, you should hear a quiet 'pop' each time. This is the sound you get when a pad seals its tone hole properly. If you don't hear a 'pop', you have a problem. Unfortunately, even if you do hear a 'pop' each time, it doesn't guarantee that the flute is perfectly sealed.

IN TUNE

To play a flute perfectly in tune, you have to adjust the pitch slightly with your embouchure as you play. The amount of adjustment necessary depends on the flute – some flutes have better tuning than others. In technical terms, the better a flute's *intonation*, the less you have to do to play it in tune.

Too high, too low

The reason you need to adjust the tuning as you play is because it isn't possible to put all the tone holes in exactly the right place for every note. This means certain notes, such as the high D-sharp, E and F-sharp, always sound too high (sharp) on a flute. You could solve this by moving the relevant tone holes slightly further down the tube – but that would make other notes sound too low (flat), such as the low C and the low D.

Scale

The intonation of a flute depends first and foremost on the positioning and size of the tone holes. This is called the *scale*. Many makers use the scale developed by the English flute-maker Albert Cooper, but some manufacturers and makers distribute the tone holes along the flute in a slightly different way. Usually the differences are only thousandths of an inch. The intonation is an important factor when you're trying out flutes, but it can be difficult to judge – if you're trying out a flute with a different scale to the instrument you're used to, the intonation may seem bad when actually it's just different.

Open hole keys and scale

Some flute-makers use a slightly different scale for their open hole flutes and their closed hole flutes. Others consider this unnecessary, which is good news for anyone who has an open hole flute with plugs in.

Venting

For a flute to sound in tune, all its keys need to seal properly and the stopper must be in the right place (see pages 81–83). The *key opening* or *pad opening* – the height of the pad cups above the tone holes – must also be properly adjusted. If the key opening is too big, the note will sound too high, and if it's too small it will sound too low. Incidentally, a slightly increased key opening can also help to make the sound a little more open and resonant, whereas a smaller key opening makes the sound slightly more warm and subdued.

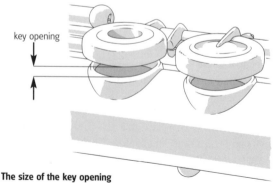

key opening

The size of the key opening affects the intonation and tone.

In tune across the whole range

If you are to hear whether a flute is adequately in tune from high to low, you need to be able to play it over that whole range. Unfortunately, if you haven't been playing very long, you'll often hear more rushing air than tone in the upper and lower notes, and you won't know whether it's the flute or your playing that is out of tune. Also it's quite difficult for an untrained ear to tell whether a note is too high or too low. So, again, if you're a beginner, it's best to take an experienced player with you when you're shopping for an instrument.

Fourths and fifths

In order to listen to a flute's intonation, most people play medium-sized *intervals* such as *fourths* (four white keys on a piano, such as from C to F) and *fifths* (five white keys, such as from C to G).

Overblowing

On a good flute, octaves can be blown easily and in tune, for instance from g' to g'' or from d' to d'' to d''', and so on. To put it another way, *overblowing* is easy on a good flute. Try playing a c' and overblowing to c'', without changing the fingering. Then play c'' with its regular fingering. Those two notes should sound exactly the same.

Narrow octaves

If the higher notes are always a little too low when you play octaves (if the octaves are *narrow*, in technical terms), your stopper may be too close to the crown. In the case of

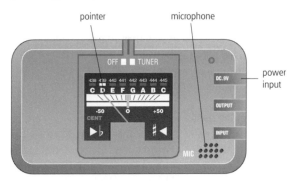

A tuner is a device which shows you exactly how high a note is

wide octaves (the high notes are too high, relative to the low ones), check whether the stopper is not too close to the mouth hole.

Tuner

An electronic tuner can be handy for checking how in or out of tune a flute is. This is a device which 'hears' which note you are playing and shows you whether it's too high, too low or exactly right.

Piccolos

It's easier to tell whether a note is out of tune when it's played on a piccolo than when it's played on a C flute or an alto flute – just as an out-of-tune violin is more likely to bother you than an out-of-tune double bass. Unfortunately, piccolos are also harder to build with good intonation than flutes.

The high B

On flutes, e''' is a difficult note to play, hence inventions such as E mechanisms and donuts. On piccolos the high B is the problem note. In fact, this note is so tricky that on some piccolos it simply cannot be played, no matter how good you are. Some players say that if you find a piccolo that you can make a high B on you should buy it at once. Others choose the piccolo they think sounds best, even if they'll never be able to play a high B on it.

A GOOD SOUND

As well as having good intonation, a flute also needs to produce a good tone. This can be hard to judge if you're new to the flute, so as already mentioned, it's a good idea to take a good player with you when you go shopping for an instrument. The following paragraphs provide some tips on testing instruments and headjoints for their sounds.

The sum of the parts

Many factors combine to determine the tone of a flute: the thickness of the wall, the weight of the material, the height of the chimney, the type of tone holes, and the length of the foot to name a few. This is why playing an instrument is the only way to judge the sound.

Somebody else

When testing flutes, it's always worth getting somebody else to play them as well as playing them yourself. This will allow you to hear the differences in tone between the various models from a distance.

Briefly at first

If you have a whole selection of flutes in front of you, choosing may be easier if you play only briefly on each one at first. Play something simple – scales, for instance, and long notes – otherwise you'll be concentrating more on playing than on listening. It may be that you prefer the sound of one of the flutes straightaway.

Two by two

Once you've limited your choice to a small selection, try comparing them two at a time. Choose the one you prefer, and swap the one which didn't match up for another. Again choose the best one, and so on. If you find, after testing instruments for a while, that it becomes very difficult to hear the differences, take a break, or come back a day or two later.

Without looking

Have a go at trying out flutes without looking to see which one you're playing. This way you can choose with your ears only, concentrating on the tone and feel without being influenced by the price, the brand name or the material of the instrument. You may find the one which you like most is the least expensive.

Sheet music

If you're used to playing from sheet music, take a few pieces with you when you go to try out some flutes. Don't take anything difficult: the easier a piece is and the better you know it, the less you'll be thinking about the notes and the more you can concentrate on the instrument. Also, bear in mind that selecting flutes works best if you have already practised that day. If you haven't played yet, the first flutes you try may sound less good than they could.

No idea

If you have no idea where to start when you walk into a

shop, ask for two very different flutes to start with. For example, comparing one with a very bright sound and another with a very warm sound is a good way to see which type of sound you prefer. Or try a very cheap flute alongside the most expensive one in the store, simply to hear how much difference it makes.

Your own flute

You may want to take your current instrument along when you go shopping for a new flute. It can certainly be interesting to compare, although you may find that you are so used to the sound and feel of your own flute that it feels better than the most expensive model in the shop.

What to listen for

Comparing sounds is something you have to learn how to do – the more often you do it, the more subtle differences you'll hear. However, it helps if you know what kind of things you should be listening out for. Here are some tips.

A matter of taste

There's no such thing as a 'perfect' flute sound. When two people listen to the same flute, they often use very different words to describe what they hear. What one person considers attractively bright and brilliant, another may consider unattractively shrill and thin. And what one regards as smooth and round, another may find dull and blunt.

The music you play

What sounds good to you is likely to depend on the kind of music you play. If you play mainly classical music, you're probably looking for a warmer, 'smaller' sound than someone who plays in a jazz group or a fife and drums corps. Sometimes players describe flutes as having an 'American character' (open sound, lots of volume), a 'French character' (elegant, flexible and light) or a 'German character' (heavy, solid, dark).

High and low

On every flute, the high notes sound different from the low ones, but the transition from high to low must be even. In other words, you should be able to hear clearly that all the notes, from high to low, are made by the same flute. The low notes shouldn't be woolly, indistinct or dull, and when you play in the highest octave, the sound shouldn't become too thin.

Loud and soft

The transition from quiet to loud and vice versa should also be even. If you start playing softly and steadily get louder a flute shouldn't suddenly sound different at one point – and yet you should be able to make it sound different if you want to. Whilst you're at it, see if you can make the low notes sound firm and whether the highest notes respond well even when you play very softly.

Projection

Listen – from a distance – to the flute's projection. A good flute can be heard right at the back of a hall, even if it's being played very softly.

Response

Especially if you're just starting out, it's important that your flute should have a good response – the notes should speak easily, so that you don't have to strain to make each one. Good players often opt for flutes which are a bit more 'difficult' or have a little more resistance; these instruments are harder work to play but generally allow for more precise control and tone colour.

The second E

Some players always start testing a flute by playing the second E (e''). If that note sounds a little 'fuzzy' or 'husky', or if it doesn't have much power or brilliance, there's a fair chance that the rest of the flute won't be too special either.

The e'' can tell you a lot about the sound of a flute.

SECONDHAND BUYING TIPS

When you go to buy a secondhand flute, there are a few things you should pay special attention to. To begin with, always put the flute together yourself, and check whether you can fit the footjoint and headjoint to the body easily, but that they aren't loose.

Leaky

If a flute has a poor response across the whole range, there's a fair chance that air is escaping. A few possible reasons: a cork stopper which has dried out and shrunk or is too far from its proper position, a leak at the seal between headjoint and body, dried-out pads, a leaking thumb key or leaking trill keys. If you're trying to locate a leak, don't try blowing cigarette smoke through the flute, as this can make the pads stick. It's better to get the instrument checked by a specialist.

Buzzes

Buzzes and other noises are easiest to find by fingering without blowing. They can be caused by many things, including torn pads, dried oil, shrivelled or missing bumpers, loose screws, worn rollers or a tuning cork plate which has come loose. However, the most common cause of buzzes is a loose crown. You can tighten a loose crown yourself easily enough, but do be careful that you don't pull the stopper out of position.

Keys

When checking the mechanism, make sure all the keys work properly (see page 40) and that they move back into place equally easily when you let go of them. If they don't, the springs may need to be replaced or adjusted, the mechanism may need to be cleaned and oiled, or certain screws may need loosening. Look out for rust patches, especially by the springs and the screws, including the screws at the ends of the rods.

From the outside

Check the whole tube for dents and other damage. The closer a dent is to the headjoint, the more effect it will have on the sound and the intonation. The headjoint itself must be completely dent-free. Even the most minor damage to the edge of the mouth hole can make a flute unplayable.

Is it solid silver?

If the ends of the headjoint and footjoint which fit inside

the body are the same colour as the rest of the flute, you're probably looking at a solid silver instrument.

A silver headjoint?

It's usually quite easy to distinguish between a silver head-joint and a silver plated one. Hold the headjoint by the crown between your thumb and index finger, and flick your nail against the tube. If you hear a ringing tone, the headjoint is silver plated; if you hear a dull 'tick' it's probably solid silver. With some headjoints, though, it's hard to tell the difference.

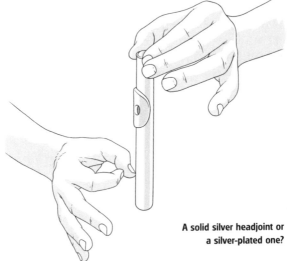

A solid silver headjoint or a silver-plated one?

Wear

You can also recognize a silver-plated flute if there are small or large patches where the silver plating has worn away. Often the first places where patches appear are the thumb key and the closed D-sharp key, because your fingers are almost always resting on them. The silver plating can also start to peel off, either because the flute was badly plated in the first place or because the previous owner had very acid perspiration. Of course, any flute can be replated (see page 101).

Nickel

Some older flutes still have nickel plating, which can cause allergic reactions (see page 34). New nickel has a different, somewhat 'harder' shine than silver. Old nickel may turn matt and greyish, but it doesn't go black or brown like silver does.

Tuning

Quite a lot of flutes produced before World War II have different tunings. In most cases that would be a lower tuning (such as A = 435 Hz) but some were made for a higher tuning (such as A = 451 Hz). These tunings are fine for playing on your own, but cause serious problems if you want to play in a group or orchestra.

Age

In order to establish the age of a flute, you need to know the serial number. You can check to see if it is marked on the flute, for example at the ends of the body or on the rib by the trill keys or the high C key. Lists of serial numbers and the accompanying years of manufacture are available from the relevant brand or on the Internet (see *Want to Know More?*, page 130).

Three places where you're likely to find the serial number

Too old?

Good flutes last a long time. You may be able to play perfectly well on an instrument thirty years old or even older, as long as it has been well reconditioned.

Cracks

Wooden flutes need to be checked for cracks. The most likely places to find cracks are the tone holes (D-sharp/E-flat especially) or the posts if it's a ribless instrument. Check the wooden headjoint for cracks, too. Cracks can be repaired, but it's very difficult to stop them reappearing. If an old wooden instrument is completely crack-free, there's a good chance it will stay that way, but you can never know for certain.

6. BEFORE AND AFTER

This chapter is about what you need to do to your flute before and after playing: from putting it together, warming up and tuning to taking it apart and drying it. You'll also find tips on transporting and amplifying your flute. Polishing, cleaning and other more serious types of maintenance are covered in Chapter 7.

Many flutes get damaged by falling out of cases opened the wrong way up. You can tell which way up your flute case is by looking at the brand name, if it's marked on the case. You can also tell by looking at the handle, which is always attached to the bottom half of a case.

Positions

Make sure you know how the headjoint, body and footjoint should be positioned in the case, so when you've finished playing you can put them back correctly. If you've forgotten, read the directions below and take a look at the illustration on the next page. The correct positions are as follows.

- The body: most of the keys should point upwards and the G-sharp lever towards you.
- The headjoint: the lip plate should point upwards, with the open end to the right.
- The footjoint: the levers should point upwards, with the non-keyed part to the left.

The body

When getting your flute out, first remove the body from the case. Place a finger against the rim at the non-keyed end and lift it up a little, using your other hand to hold the other end in place. Then take hold of the body by the end furthest from the keys. Take the headjoint out of the case in the same way and slide it into the body with a careful twisting movement.

The lip plate

Never hold the headjoint by the lip plate – if you do you risk bending it, and grease from your fingers will end up in the mouth hole. Also, if you wear a ring, you can easily damage the edge of the mouth hole with it.

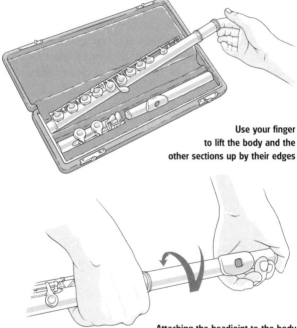

Use your finger to lift the body and the other sections up by their edges

Attaching the headjoint to the body

Marks

The headjoint must be positioned so that the centre of the mouth hole is in line with the keys. The illustration below shows how it should look. On some flutes, the correct position of the headjoint is indicated by small guide marks.

Everything in line: the mouth hole, the keys of the body and the key rod of the footjoint

Footjoint and body

The key rod on the footjoint must also be aligned with the keys on the body. The easiest way to achieve this is to use the centre of the D key as a guide. Lift the footjoint out of the case in the same way as the body and slide it into the body with a careful twisting movement. If your fingers are strong enough and your flute is well maintained, you'll be able to do this while holding the footjoint by its end, again avoiding holding the keywork.

More grip

If you need more grip, take hold of the footjoint with your whole hand. Hold it in such a way that the soft cushions on the undersides of your fingers lie across the keys and key rods.

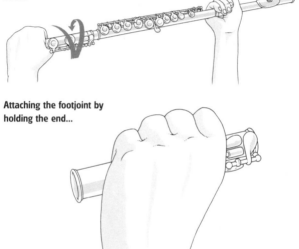

Attaching the footjoint by
holding the end...

...and by using your whole hand

Headjoint first

It's best to put the headjoint on before the footjoint because the footjoint is often a bit trickier to attach. If the headjoint is already fitted, it gives you more to hold onto.

No grease, no polish

If assembling your flute takes too much force, clean the *tenons* (the ends which slide inside the other tubes) with a dry cloth. Don't wet or grease them, as dust and dirt clings to grease and moisture, causing scratches. And don't use silver polish or other types of polish, because you'll remove too much material, and this will make the joint loose. If a dry cloth doesn't do the trick, get an expert to look at the instrument.

Sleeves

Occasionally flutes come with a metal sleeve, meant to supply some extra protection for the open end of the headjoint when the instrument is taken to bits. However, these caps are often a cause of additional wear and scratches, as they need to be put on and taken off every time you get out your flute.

Assembling a piccolo

To remove a piccolo from its case, take hold of the top end of the body – the non-keyed part. Hold it by the same end when you attach the headjoint, which should be done with a gentle twisting movement. As with a flute, the mouth hole must be aligned with the keys.

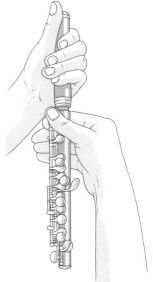

More grip

If you need more grip, make sure the keys are pointing upwards and take hold of the body in such a way that the soft cushions on the undersides of your fingers lie across the keys and key rods.

How to assemble a piccolo

Leave room between two fingers for the G-sharp lever so that you don't put any pressure on it.

Cork grease

The cork rings on some wooden instruments (see the top illustration on page 62) occasionally need a touch of special *cork grease*, which you can buy in most music stores. This keeps the rings intact longer, creates a better seal and makes the instrument easier to assemble. The cork rings on a new instrument will often not have been greased so they don't appear dirty.

Inwards, outwards
Instead of aligning the mouth hole exactly with the keys, you can choose to twist the headjoint slightly. If you keep your hands in the same position, twisting the headjoint will alter how much of the mouth hole you cover, affecting the sound and the volume. If you twist the headjoint but play with your mouth in the same position, it will effect your posture and balance.

Nail varnish
Once you've determined the best headjoint position for sound and comfort, you may want to mark it by putting two small dots of coloured nail varnish next to each other on the flute – one on the headjoint and one on the body. This way you can quickly return to the same position in the future by aligning the dots.

Hands and teeth
Playing when you've just eaten or drunk a fizzy drink can lead to sticky pads and a dirty instrument. If you have just eaten, rinse your mouth out – or ideally brush your teeth – before playing. And if you want to polish your flute as little as possible, which is best for your instrument, wash your hands before playing.

TUNING
When you're playing with others, you always need to tune your instrument before you start. When playing alone, you can skip tuning – but the more often you tune your flute, the quicker and more accurate you'll become at it and the sooner you'll learn how to play in tune.

Longer is lower
More than anything else, learning to tune properly means learning to listen carefully, and this comes with practice. Tuning itself isn't very hard – you lower the tuning of a flute by pulling the headjoint out of the body slightly. This makes the tube longer, and a longer tube gives a lower tone.

If you push the headjoint further in, the tube becomes shorter and so the tone becomes higher. The headjoint's tenon is sometimes referred to as the *tuning slide*.

Pianos and tuning forks

Most instruments are tuned to the note a' (see page 12). Rather than using a piano or other keyboard instrument to find that note, you can use a *tuning fork*: a thick metal fork which you tap against your knee before putting next to your ear to hear the note. Standard tuning forks produce a 440 hertz A, but because certain ensembles use slightly different tuning (see page 55) tuning forks of different pitches are also available, such as those which produce a 442 hertz or a 444 hertz A.

A tuning fork – the pitch indication (440 hertz) is shown on the stem

Metronomes and tuners

Many electronic metronomes and tuners can also produce a 440 hertz A, sometimes adjustable to higher or lower tunings.

Compare the notes

Listen carefully to the A produced by the piano or tuning fork and then play the A on your flute. If the note you play sounds a little higher, pull the headjoint out a tiny bit. If it sounds lower, you need to push it in slightly. Most flutes are properly tuned when the headjoint is pulled out about a tenth of an inch (around 2–3mm). You tune a piccolo in the same way as a flute, only it sounds an octave higher.

Other notes

Because certain notes have a tendency to always sound a little too high (*sharp*) or too low (*flat*), many players use several notes when tuning. They may go from the A to a higher and a lower E, for example, play some high A notes as well as the low one, or listen to various other notes from a piece they are going to play – all the time listening to how each of those notes sounds compared to the others.

Your flute is ideally tuned if you can play as many notes as possible in tune with as little effort as possible.

To G
Some players prefer to tune to G because they think the instrument ends up more in tune that way – but in most orchestras and groups you only get an A to tune to.

The warmer, the higher
After you have been playing for a few minutes, you'll notice the instrument getting warmer, which can cause the tuning to go up slightly – especially if you have a metal piccolo. That means you have to adjust the tuning by pulling the headjoint out a little more. Many players warm their instrument up before tuning, to save them having to readjust it. The quickest way to do this is to blow into the instrument with your mouth covering the entire mouth hole, while closing all the tone holes.

Playing outdoors
If you are playing outdoors and the temperature rises, the chances are your tuning will rise too. That means you'll have to pull the headjoint out a little further than you would normally. And if the temperature drops, the tuning goes down, so you push the headjoint in a little bit instead.

Warming up wood
Temperature has much less effect on the tuning of wooden and plastic instruments. Even so, wooden flutes and piccolos also need to be warmed up before being played. If you skip this step and blow warm, moist air straight into a cold, dry wooden flute, you increase the chances of it cracking. The easiest way to warm the headjoint or the whole instrument (if it's a piccolo) is simply to hold it in your hands. If it's cold outside, don't unpack your instrument straight away when you go indoors. It will have more time to get used to the higher temperature in its case.

THE STOPPER
When a flute is tuned, the headjoint is usually only pulled out about a tenth of an inch. If you need to pull it out much further than that, the stopper may be out of position.

The right position

In order to be able to tune up and play in tune, the stopper must be in exactly the right place, and this can be checked with a cleaning rod. Most cleaning rods have a notch towards the end – if you carefully insert the cleaning rod into the headjoint until it touches the stopper, the notch should be exactly in the centre of the mouth hole.

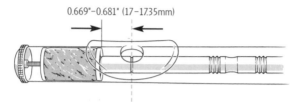

0.669"–0.681" (17–17.35mm)

The notch in the cleaning rod should be exactly in the centre of the mouth hole

Too far up

If the notch is too far to the left, your stopper is too far up towards the crown. This is very common as the vibrations of a flute can make the crown come loose now and again. If you turn it even slightly too far when you tighten it, the crown pulls the stopper up a little bit. The solution is simple: unscrew the crown slightly and push it back into the headjoint until the cork is in the correct position.

Too far down

If the stopper is too far down, pull it out a little by carefully pulling the crown. Then gently tighten the crown. If you can't unscrew the crown with your fingers, or you have to use much force to move the cork, take your flute to a repairer.

Too easily

If the stopper moves out of place very easily, it needs to be replaced. Many repairers will do that anyway when over-hauling or even just adjusting an instrument.

Narrow octaves

If the stopper is too far up, the flute is slightly longer than it should be. As a result, all the notes will sound slightly too low. The high notes are more affected by this than the low ones, which means that the octaves become narrow (see page 67). If the cork is too far down, the octaves will be wide.

The right place

To be precise, the stopper must be between 0.669" and 0.681" (17 and 17.3 mm) to the left of the centre of the mouth hole. That distance is exactly the same as the inside diameter of the tube at that point. The corresponding distance on a piccolo is 0.295" (7.5 mm) and on an alto flute 1.02" (26 mm). Naturally, cleaning rods for those instruments have notches at the appropriate points.

AFTER PLAYING

When you play, the moisture in your breath condenses and makes the inside of your flute slightly wet. And the outside of the flute collects dirt and sweat from your fingertips, which can harm the silver or silver plating. So, it's a good idea to dry and clean your instrument after playing. This only takes a few minutes.

Drying

Remove the headjoint and footjoint from the flute in the same way that you attached them, and lay all three sections in the case. Take them out, one by one, to dry them

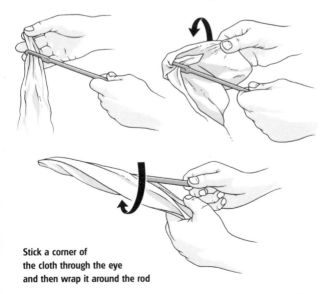

Stick a corner of
the cloth through the eye
and then wrap it around the rod

on the inside with a cotton cloth wrapped around the cleaning rod. Most players use an ordinary handkerchief. Stick a corner of the cloth through the eye of the cleaning rod and twist it around the rod as shown in the illustration.

The footjoint...
To dry the footjoint, push the cleaning rod through it a few times. If you pull it backwards and forwards you may damage the pads.

...the body...
Do the same thing with the body. If you push the cleaning rod all the way in, you can pull it through from the other end. If you can't reach it properly, push it a bit further in with your finger. As ever, hold the flute by the non-keyed end when drying it.

...and the headjoint
Drying the headjoint is easier if you first pull the cloth a bit further through the eye in the cleaning rod to make a kind of 'brush', as shown in the following illustration. This makes it easier to reach deep inside the headjoint.

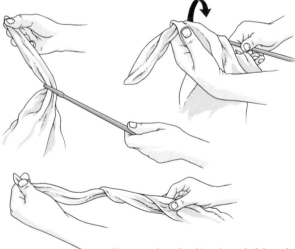

How to make a 'brush' at the end of the rod

Pull, push and twist
Another way to clean the headjoint is to leave the cloth as it was before. Stick the cleaning rod and cloth inside the

headjoint a short distance, pull the rod back a little way and then push it back in whilst twisting gently. Repeat the process (pull, push, twist) until the cloth just touches the stopper. Make sure you don't push the cork out of place.

Tips

- A handkerchief that has been washed many times works much better than a new one.
- Don't store the cloth with the flute (and certainly not inside the flute), unless your case has a separate, well-sealed-off compartment for it.
- Wash the cloth now and then. It does get dirty after a while.

Swab

A flute swab, a piece of chamois leather that you pull through a flute with a string, is an alternative way to clean the body and the footjoint (but not the headjoint).

A flute swab

Silk

Players with wooden flutes often opt for a silk cloth or swab. If you can't find a silk swab in the flute section of a music shop, try the oboe section, as oboe swabs can be used for flutes too.

Padsaver

A padsaver is a long fluffy plume which you stick into your flute after drying it to absorb any remaining moisture. The drawback of padsavers is that they can leave fibres in the instrument, which can cause leaks. Always use a padsaver in combination with a cloth or a swab, not instead of one, and never leave a padsaver in a flute after use.

During breaks

Even if you only stop playing for short while, it's still a good idea to dry your flute. The more often and the better you dry it, the longer your pads will last.

The outside

Wipe the outside of your flute (and the tenons) with a soft, dry, lint-free cloth. Rubbing softly is usually enough, but make sure you remove the fingerprints. Don't use a silver-polishing cloth for this daily cleaning, especially not if you have a silver-plated flute (see page 92).

Holding the flute

Again, always grip the parts of the flute where there are no keys. You can also clean the outside while the cloth and cleaning rod are still inside the flute. That way you can hold the cleaning rod instead of the instrument. Sit at a table when you are cleaning your flute so that it doesn't fall as far if you drop it.

Force, grease and tools

If you can't get the headjoint or footjoint loose, don't grip them extra hard, don't use oil or grease and never use a wrench or other tools. Wrap the flute in a towel (it won't fit inside its case anymore) and take it to a repairer.

On the table

If you are taking a break from playing, put your instrument on a table or another flat surface where it can't fall, and always lay it down with the keys pointing upwards.

Stands

If you don't like leaving your flute lying around, you could get a flute stand, which shouldn't cost you more than

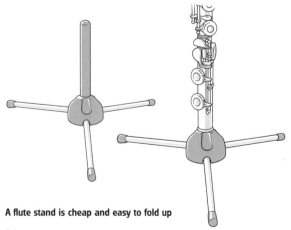

A flute stand is cheap and easy to fold up

around £10/$15. However, many players hate stands, because they are very easy to knock over, especially when they have a flute on them. If you do want to buy a stand, check how easily the legs fold up, and if you really want to look after your flute, go for one with a felt-covered peg.

In the case

If you stop playing for a while, pack your flute away. Your flute is safest in its case, and it'll also keep its shine better. Solid silver flutes especially are liable to tarnish quickly if they aren't kept in their cases. What's more, pads can dry out, moths can eat the felt in the pads and dust is bad for the mechanism.

Never

Never lay a flute on a chair, bed or bench. And never put a flute on or near a heater or a radiator, or any place that gets very hot, even if it's in its case. Heat can make pads dry out and cause the mechanism to expand slightly and become sluggish as a result. Wooden flutes can crack if they get too warm, and they can be damaged by being laid on something cold too.

Walking along

If you're walking along with your flute in your hand, hold it vertically in front of you so that it doesn't hit people, furniture or other obstacles; hold it by the body, avoiding the keywork. Never hold it by the headjoint or footjoint as the rest of the flute may fall off as you walk.

On the road

Keeping your flute safe when you're out and about is mainly just a matter of common sense. Make sure it's always in sight when you're on a train or coach, for example, and never leave it on the back shelf of a car where it can be clearly seen and exposed to direct sunlight. And if you're flying with your flute, make sure you carry it in your hand luggage. However, you should also look into insuring your instrument.

Insurance

Depending on their value, musical instruments usually fall into the category of 'valuables' for home insurance. This means you have to let your insurance company know you have an instrument in order for it to be covered. Some home insurance policies also allow you to take out extra cover for your instrument to protect it when you take it out of the house. This can be quite expensive, but it means the instrument will be covered against theft and damage, whether you're on the road, at a practice or on stage. Some insurance companies also do specific policies for musicians.

Serial number

Note down the serial number of your flute, as it may be required by your insurance company or the police if the instrument is ever stolen or lost. There's a form to do this on page 132. And keep your proof of purchase, as this may also be required.

CASES AND CASE COVERS

Cases come in many different types and materials. Most flutes are sold complete with case, and sometimes even a case cover.

French and modern

The classic case is made of wood and covered with leather or synthetic leather. 'French style' cases don't have handles. The inside is often made of shock-absorbent material, with

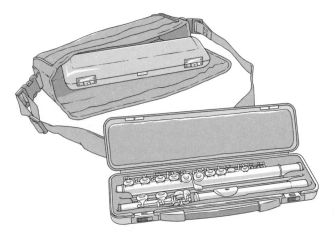

A flute in a case, a case in a cover

a soft lining made of velvet or another fabric. The modern version has a hard shell made of a synthetic material which is more resilient and less heavy than wood.

Locks
The lids of cases are often closed with metal fasteners. Ones which click shut by themselves are safest for your instrument. Lock the fasteners if you can – then the flute won't fall out if you ever drop the case.

Soft cases
Other cases are made entirely of soft material with a water-repellent layer on the outside. These soft-sided flute cases or *gig bags* often have extra compartments for a cleaning rod, a stand and the like, and straps so you can carry them over your shoulder. They usually close with a zip.

Case covers
The easiest way to carry a traditional hard-shell case is to use a case cover. Most case covers provide extra protection against rain and some are padded, making your flute less vulnerable to knocks and bumps, as well as changes of temperature (which is especially important for wooden flutes). Case covers come in leather, canvas or synthetic materials, and with or without compartments, handles or reinforced corners. An adjustable and detachable shoulder strap is always handy.

More cases
Special flute bags are also available, with compartments for a flute case and a piccolo case, for a stand, sheet music, a metronome and more. You can also get a combination case which fits a flute and a piccolo, or a special case with room for two headjoints, for example.

Prices
The simplest cases are available for as little as £20/$30, going up with quality. When choosing a case, try out fastenings and zips for sturdiness.

Cleaning rod
Not every case has room for a cleaning rod. If yours doesn't, you can keep the rod in the case cover. Some people

store their wooden or plastic cleaning rods inside their flutes – but never do this with a metal cleaning rod.

MICROPHONES

If you want to play in a band, your flute will probably need amplification. You can use an ordinary microphone, but special flute microphone systems are also available. Connecting your flute to a sound system allows you to not only increase the volume but also to influence the sound by adding effects such as reverb, chorus or delay (echo).

Vocal microphones

A good vocal microphone will work fine for a flute. However, if you're playing with a mike on a traditional stand, moving backwards and forwards will change your your volume level and sound. This can be used as an effect, but it forces you to keep quite still when you play.

Flute microphones

To overcome this, several manufacturers make special holders which allow you to attach small condenser microphones – usually designed especially for the flute – to your instrument. Most systems work with a single microphone right above the mouth hole. To allow you to place it where it picks up as much tone and as little noise as possible, it is mounted on a flexible metal wire or a so-called *goose-neck* or *swan-neck*. Other systems have a second mike on the footjoint. Prices are around £75–£350/$100–$500, though you may pay even more for a good cordless system.

Pre-amplifier

Most flute microphones come with a pre-amplifier to boost the signal before it's sent to the main amplifier. Most pre-amplifiers are small enough to be clipped to a belt or put in a pocket, and some have volume and tone controls.

Headsets

Musicians who sometimes sing as well as playing often use a *headset*: a microphone attached to a strap which fits over the head. Some flute players use one of these instead of a special flute microphone. The cheapest headsets cost around £50/$75.

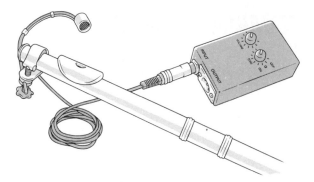

A flute microphone with clamp and pre-amplifier (SD Systems)

Buying tips

A few microphone buying tips:

- Some pre-amplifiers have a tone control as well as a volume control.
- Clamp systems vary in the way they are attached to the flute, how securely they fit and how easy they are to adjust.
- If possible, try out the various systems with the same amplifier and at the same volume, and switch off effects like reverb.
- Some systems use a detachable cable between the microphone and the pre-amplifier. Others have an integral cable, which is harder to replace if it causes interference, crackle or simply doesn't work.

Batteries and cables

Pre-amplifiers run on batteries – always take a spare with you when you're playing away from home. And take a spare cable, too, if your system uses a detachable cable.

7. MAINTENANCE

If you do everything mentioned in the last chapter every time you use your flute, it probably won't need much more maintenance. Just an extra polish now and again, maybe the odd drop of oil once in a while, and perhaps an occasional bit of pad surgery. This chapter explains what you can do to maintain your instrument, and what you should leave to a professional.

If you wipe your metal flute with a soft, dry cloth every time you finish playing and pack it away at once, you'll only rarely need to polish it. When you do, use a silver-polishing cloth or mitts, which you can buy in most music stores for £3/$5 or less. These remove tarnish, minor discolouring and fingerprints, and most also leave behind a very thin protective layer.

Black
A silver-polishing cloth gets steadily blacker the more you use it. This isn't just dirt, it's also the silver you remove from your flute to make the silver below shine through. If you have a silver-plated instrument, you should only polish it once every few months at most. The silver plating is only about a thousandth of an inch thick (a few hundredth of a millimetre), and if you polish too often, you'll wear right through it.

Two tips
You only need to replace a silver polishing cloth if it stops polishing properly – not just because it gets black. In fact, usually, the blacker a cloth gets, the better it will work. And

never wash a sliver-polishing cloth, as this will make it useless.

Nooks and crannies

Only use a silver-polishing cloth for the parts you can reach easily – don't try to squeeze it under keys, key rods and springs. Wrapping the cloth around a small screwdriver to get to the difficult bits is not a good idea. There are special brushes to get the dust out of these nooks and crannies, and some ordinary small, soft brushes may be fine too. If you're using a cotton bud, make sure no fibres end up in the mechanism or under the pads.

Pads, pins and springs

Keep away from the keys when you are polishing; the edges of the pads will wear through quickly if the cloth keeps rubbing past them. And be careful not to cut your fingers on the sharp needle springs or the pins. Check that everything still works after you finish polishing – the springs by the upper trill keys are especially easy to pull loose by accident.

Keys

Because keys can be bent out of place very easily, it's better not to polish them yourself. Leave it to a repairer, who will polish the keys when you take your flute for cleaning, oiling and adjusting, or for an overhaul.

Silver polish

Don't use silver polish or any other heavy-duty metal polishes that aren't meant for musical instruments. They are very abrasive, and you can easily remove too much material if you use them, even if you have a solid silver flute. What's more, residue from the polish can get inside the mechanism or under your pads. If you can't get a flute shiny with a silver-polishing cloth, it's a lot safer to get it looked at by an expert.

Dirty headjoints

All headjoints eventually get dirty inside, even if you always play with freshly brushed teeth. The best way to tackle the inside of the headjoint is to clean it very carefully with a cotton bud and a few drops of rubbing alcohol (you can

get this from a chemist or drugstore) or a little detergent
and a soft brush, such as a toothbrush or a special headjoint cleaner.

Without the stopper
You can also clean a headjoint – but no other part of the
flute – with water. First unscrew the crown, then carefully
push the stopper down past the mouth hole and out of the
headjoint. The headjoint is slightly narrower at the other
end (by the crown), so you'll never get it out that way. If
you can't shift the cork, take the headjoint to a repairer.

Under the tap
Once you've got the stopper out, you can rinse out the
headjoint under the tap with lukewarm water.

Really dirty
If your headjoint is really dirty, with hard deposits on the
inside, don't clean it yourself but get a professional to do it.

Playing
When you're polishing, check the mechanism too. Are all
the keys equally easy to play and do they all return to their
positions equally quickly? Is there any play in the keys
(very carefully, see if they move from side to side)? Do you
hear any rattles or buzzes when you finger the keys?

Medicines and eggs
Some people claim that taking certain medicines and
eating eggs or certain vegetables (such as spinach) can
result in a discoloured flute. However, most players don't
find this.

Rashes and discolouring
Some players get blisters or rashes on their chin or lip
from touching the lip plate, especially if it's nickel plated.
Solid silver lip plates may discolour badly even though you
don't suffer any reaction. You may also notice discoloured
or dull patches where your right thumb and left index finger touch the flute, especially on solid silver instruments.
One way to solve these problems is to get the lip plate, the
head or even the whole flute gold plated (see page 101),
but there are also a few things you can try yourself first.

Nail varnish and masking tape

Some players apply a very thin layer of clear nail varnish to the lip plate – of course you must make sure none gets onto the edge of the mouth hole or inside it. Others stick a piece of masking tape or cotton plaster onto the lip plate. And you can try either nail varnish or masking tape for the spots where your fingers discolour the tube. Masking tape and plasters are less smooth than silver, so they also give you a little more grip, making it less likely that you'll drop the flute. Don't try using a postage stamp instead, as the glue adheres too well, and may even be bad for the metal. And if you use tape or plaster, replace it from time to time: the longer you leave it there, the harder it will be to get off.

The mechanism

If you start fiddling with the mechanism, you'll soon find that a flute is more complicated than it looks, which is why adjustments to this bit of the instrument are best left to a pro. If a key rod is loose, or if your instrument vibrates when you play, it may be that the screw at the end of the rod (the *pivot screw*) is loose or missing.

Leaks

Leaks usually happen very gradually, so you can easily fail to notice that you're having to press the keys down harder and harder. If you get someone else to play your instrument now and again, they won't be used to having to press harder to close leaking keys, so will be more likely to notice that a pad is no longer sealing properly. While you're polishing and checking your flute, take some time to test it for leaks (see page 65).

Oil

Music stores sell special cleaning sets for flutes. Besides a flute swab, a silver-polishing cloth, a brush for the mechanism and a headjoint cleaner, they often include a small bottle of key oil. Some manufacturers advise you to put a tiny drop of oil on the hinges every month or two.

Don't do it yourself

Many flute repairers prefer players not to oil a flute them- selves, because extra oil only really helps if you first take the mechanism apart and clean it completely. There's also a risk that you'll use too much oil, get oil on the pads or use oil that is too thick or too runny for your flute. So if you want to be on the safe side, leave it to an expert. Once a year or every six months is usually enough if it's done properly.

Doing it yourself

If you do decide to do the oiling yourself, apply the oil with a pin. A good technique is to put a drop of oil onto a cigarette paper and dip your pin into it – this way you'll never get too much oil on the pin. Some bottles come with a pin on the nozzle, but these often give out too much oil at once.

Special oil

Always use special key oil, not sewing machine oil or any other kind of household oil you may happen to have.

Mute

Compared to an expensive instrument, a cheap flute will always have slightly more 'space' in its mechanism, for instance between one key rod and a second which fits inside it. In this case, as well as lubricating the parts, the oil serves to mute any sound the mechanism may make. If you hear soft metal-on-metal sounds when you play, your flute probably needs oiling. Generally, the better a flute's construction, the less oil it will need.

Loose and broken springs

If a spring comes loose when you're cleaning your flute, you'll often be able to put it back in place yourself. The easiest way is with a crochet needle, but you may even be able to do it with your fingers. If a spring breaks on one of the *inactive keys* (the keys which are closed when you're not playing: trill keys, G-sharp and D-sharp), you can use a rubber band to keep it closed as a temporary measure. But do remove it as soon as you stop playing, as rubber is harmful to silver.

Sluggish keys

If a key is sluggish or doesn't open at all and you don't hear any odd noises, something is probably bent, or the mechanism needs lubricating, or the spring needs to be adjusted or replaced. These are all jobs for a repairer. If you hear a 'sticky' sound when a key opens, it's probably because the pad is momentarily sticking to the edge of the tone hole.

STICKY PADS

All players occasionally get sticky pads, but it's likely to be more of a problem if you eat or drink anything containing a lot of sugar before you play, if you don't dry your flute after playing, or if you blow a lot of moisture into your flute – some players have 'wetter' breath than others.

The closed keys

The pads of the inactive keys tend to stick more easily than the other pads. This isn't just because they are always closed when you're not playing, but also because they are lower down in the tube, so the moisture in the flute always runs towards them (they're in the 'spit track').

Cigarette papers

You can usually fix a sticky pad yourself by using a cigarette paper: the follwing paragraphs show you how. However, some repairers advice against this technique, so you may want to speak to your teacher or repairer before proceding.

Between pad and tone hole

If you can only find gummed papers, tear off the gummed edge. Slide the cigarette paper between the pad and the tone hole, and carefully close the pad cup a few times by tapping it with a fingertip. If there's no improvement, insert a clean cigarette paper and gently hold the pad cup closed a little while (don't move it to and fro).

Lighter fuel or alcohol

If there's still no improvement, take another clean cigarette paper, moisten it with one or two drops of lighter fuel or rubbing alcohol (both of which are highly flammable) and repeat the above steps, several times if necessary. Then repeat once more with a dry cigarette paper to make sure the pad is completely dry.

Moving the paper

If you don't have any lighter fuel to hand and dry cigarette papers aren't helping, gently hold the pad cup closed and give the cigarette paper a few short, gentle tugs, preferably without pulling it from between pad and tone hole completely. Try pulling in various directions, using a clean paper each time. Be careful, though: if you do this too often or pull too hard, you may end up having to replace the pads altogether – even cigarette papers are very coarse for the ultra-thin membrane which covers the pads.

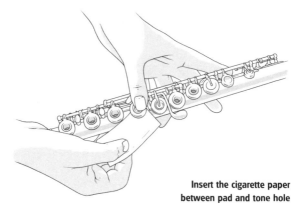

Insert the cigarette paper between pad and tone hole

Wait and see

Any method you use to clean your pads will cause some wear. So never clean a pad unless it's actually sticking. Also, sticking pads sometimes cure themselves, so many players always wait for a while before cleaning them.

Things to avoid

There are various techniques used by some players on their pads which are not good for an instrument. For example, talcum powder can alleviate the stickiness of a pad for a while, but not for very long. And once you start playing, the powder gets damp, which actually makes everything stick even worse. What's more, because talcum powder is so fine, it can easily find its way into the mechanism, where it can mix with the oil to form a sticky mess. Other things to avoid are other kinds of powder, chalk, paper tissues, newsprint, paper which is too thick (such as the paper of this book), paper which is too coarse (such as banknotes), and fluids other than lighter fuel or rubbing alcohol.

Damp pads

The pads of a piccolo's trill keys can sometimes become so damp that the moisture closes off the tone holes when you release the keys. Damp pads are easily dried with a cigarette paper. If you have a new instrument, you may find that you have more trouble with damp pads than you did on your old one. Often the problem takes care of itself once the flute has been used for a while and the edges of the tone holes are no longer spotlessly clean.

WOODEN FLUTES

There are few things that flute players disagree about as strongly as the oiling of the inside of wooden flutes.

Cracks

Most experts believe that a thin film of oil slightly reduces the effects of temperature and moisture, lessening the chances of cracks appearing. Others say grenadilla wood is so hard that oil can't penetrate it, which means it can't prevent cracking. Either way, wooden flutes do sometimes crack, whether or not they are regularly treated with oil.

Non-drying oil

The most common type of oil used on wooden flutes is sweet almond oil, which you can buy from a health food shop or drugstore. As an alternative, you could use good olive oil or peanut oil, but they both have a stronger smell. Some experts say that the drawback of all these three types is that they don't dry. So, if you pull a cloth through the flute after playing, you wipe the oil off again.

Drying oil

Linseed oil does dry and so does tung oil, which has a weaker smell and is less likely to produce allergic reactions. These 'hard' oil types are best applied by an expert, because if you use a bit too much you can end up with a crusty, gel-like layer inside your flute.

Reducing resistance

Some experts claim these drying oils, as well as possibly reducing the chance of cracking, fill up the pores and the grain of the wood, making the inside of the instrument smoother and in turn reducing the flute's resistance and making it more playable.

Only the headjoint

Theobald Boehm recommended that flute players should oil the headjoint but not the body and the footjoint. Many flute-makers agree – they say the body should only be treated with oil if the mechanism has been removed, because otherwise oil may get on the pads. Other manufacturers see no problem with oiling the body and the footjoint. These companies usually advise you to apply a tiny amount of oil to the inside of a new flute about once a month. Used flutes don't need to be oiled as often.

Not the headjoint

Some flute-makers and repairers think you shouldn't even oil the headjoint, because a greasy headjoint gets dirty inside more easily. If you do decide to oil your headjoint or body, use as little oil as possible dripped onto a cotton cloth wrapped around your cleaning rod. It's a good idea to ask the advice of a repairer or the person who sold you your flute before you start.

SERVICE AND OVERHAULS

All other maintenance, adjustments and repairs are best left to a professional.

New flutes

A new flute needs to be completely checked and adjusted after a year, if not sooner. Sometimes that first service is included in the price.

Cleaning, oiling and adjusting

If you play about half an hour a day and you get your flute checked once a year, you can be fairly sure nothing major will go wrong. Some repairers think once every two years is enough. Basic servicing of the instrument (cleaning, oiling and adjusting) usually costs around £50/$75, but the longer you wait, the more expensive it can get.

Overhauls

Once every five or ten years, almost every flute is ready for an overhaul or reconditioning, depending on how good the instrument is, how much it's been played and how well it's been maintained. An overhaul includes replacing the pads. Prices usually start at around £200/$300, but the cost can be much less or much more, depending on how much work needs to be done and on the quality and age of the flute, among other things. After a professional reconditioning job, even a cheap flute may play and sound better than it did when it was new, and it will probably last a good few years longer without much additional expense.

Gold and silver plating

If you want to have a flute gold plated or you want the silver plating renewed, have it done as part of the overhaul, as the repairer will take the instrument apart then anyway.

8. BACK IN TIME

The oldest flute ever found, made out of a bear's bone, is around forty-five thousand years old. *Transverse flutes* **(flutes played sideways) are much more recent, and the modern flute only dates from 1847. Here's a brief history of the flute in a few pages.**

The Chinese *chi'ih*, used at least three thousand years ago, was probably one of the very first transverse flutes. However, the instrument seems to have disappeared quite soon after that time, and only much later, around 1100 AD, did the transverse flute crop up again, mainly in Germany. Nobody knows for certain what happened to the flute in the centuries in between these times.

The army
During the Middle Ages, most flutes were made of wood with six tone holes and no keys. A small model, the *fife*, was used in the army together with one or more drums.

Renaissance flutes
By the start of the sixteenth century there were three standard sizes of flute – alto, tenor and bass – though others such as the high descant also existed. Players of these *Renaissance flutes* often accompanied singers, or they played in groups with other musicians.

One key: the traversa
It was probably a Frenchman (either Hotteterre or Philibert) who gave the flute its first key, sometime after 1680. It was a D-sharp key which was operated with the right little

finger, just like on a modern flute. Other changes were also made to the flute around this time: the tube was made steadily narrower towards the end and it was divided into three sections (the headjoint, the body and the footjoint with the one key on it). The resulting instrument was the *traversa* or *Baroque flute* (see the illustration on the following page). A little later, similar flutes appeared with a second key beside the first.

Baroque flute music

By the first half of the eighteenth century, pieces were regularly written for the flute – by such composers as Vivaldi, Bach, Telemann and the German flute-maker and player Quantz. Many musicians still prefer to play music from this period on instruments similar to the traversas of the time. You can buy modern copies of these old flutes; they are usually constructed of wood, like the originals, but also come in plastic.

More keys

On a traversa you can only play in tune in a few keys. In order to be able to play in different keys and together with other instruments, additional keys were needed. Around 1760 the first flutes were made with four keys (D-sharp, F, G-sharp and B-flat), and not much later instruments with six, eight or even more keys appeared, such as the nine-key flute pictured over the page.

Theobald Boehm

There was still lots of room for improvement, though, at least in the opinion of the German flute player and goldsmith Theobald Boehm (1794–1881). He wanted to build flutes which could be played in tune in every key, and which would produce more volume and a better tone. His solution was to change the size and position of the tone holes and add a key system which allowed the player to operate sixteen tone holes with just nine fingers.

The Boehm flute

Boehm was in his late thirties when he produced his first 'improved' flute – a wooden, conical *ring-key flute*, similar to the one shown on page 105. Around fifteen years later, in 1847, he built the first modern flute: the silver, cylindrical

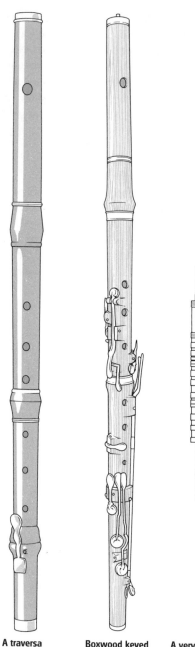

A traversa

Boxwood keyed
flute with nine keys

A very different flute,
which nonetheless
works in the same
way (Matit)

instrument which still bears his name. He used silver because he thought it sounded better and offered more tonal scope than wood, and he gave the flute a cylindrical tube as this provided a richer, more resonant tone than a conical tube.

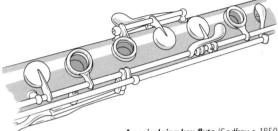

A conical ring-key flute (Godfroy c..1850)

Briccialdi

Only one major addition has been made to the 1847 Boehm flute: the B-flat lever for the left thumb. This was one of three systems which Boehm later devised for that thumb, though Italian Giulio Briccialdi improved on it and is often credited with its invention, which is why it's often known as the *Briccialdi B-flat lever*.

More volume

Apart from that, today's flutes look almost exactly the same as those of a hundred and fifty years ago. Extra trill keys, special mechanisms and rubber stoppers have been added, but there have been no changes to the basic design. Even so, an old flute does play differently from a new one. New flutes usually play more easily and produce more volume, partly because the mouth hole and tone holes have become slightly bigger.

Flutes in the future

There's every chance that flutes will look almost identical in 100 years' time. At present there are very few flute-makers willing to take on the challenge of building a completely new type of flute, but there are some, such as the makers of the Matit flute (pictured on the previous page). This is an expensive flute with an ultra-light carbon-fibre tube, magnets instead of springs, plastic pads and a right-hand mechanism which has been moved to the other side of the flute so that it never gets in the way.

9. THE FAMILY

There are many more members of the flute family than just the Boehm flute, the piccolo, the alto and the bass flute. Contrabass flutes for example, and flutes which are played in a very different way. And of course the flute is also related to all the other woodwind instruments.

The most common flutes can be divided into three groups: fipple flutes, transverse flutes and vertical flutes.

Fipple flutes

The best-known example of a *fipple flute* is the recorder. You place your lips around the beak-shaped mouthpiece and when you blow the air is directed towards the edge by a *duct*. This explains why this type of flute is also known as a *duct-flute*.

Transverse flutes

On a transverse or *side-blown* flute, you have to direct the airstream yourself. This is harder to learn, but it gives you more control over the sound. There are lots of types of transverse flutes besides those discussed in this book, including many from India and the Far East made of bamboo, wood or other materials. Many of these instruments are available in the West.

Vertical flutes

To play a *vertical* or *end-blown flute* you also direct the air yourself, blowing across the top much as you would the top of a bottle. A panpipe is really a bunch of end-blown flutes stuck together. The Turkish or Egyptian *nay* or *ney flute* and the Balkan *kaval* also belong to this branch of the flute family.

Many more

There are also many other types of flutes, including *globular flutes* (such as the small, egg-shaped *ocarina*), flutes you play by blowing through your nose, and flutes with two or more tubes which you sound at the same time.

DIFFERENT SIZES

This book is mainly about the instrument we usually refer to simply as the flute (or C flute, Boehm flute, soprano flute, concert flute, etc), but it also covers the smaller piccolo and the alto and bass flutes. However, the modern flute also comes in various other shapes, sizes and keys.

Contrabass flute

The *contrabass flute* is even bigger and deeper than the bass flute, and a few makers even produce a *sub-contrabass flute*, which can go almost as low as a piano. A sub-contrabass flute, which makes a very soft sound, is almost six feet tall, and if you were to roll it out it would be more than fifteen feet long. Contra and sub-contrabass flutes are very rare and very expensive – even an 'ordinary' bass flute usually cost at least £2000/ $3000.

PVC

Because these super-low flutes are so expensive, some makers offer cheaper alternatives. For example, the bass and contrabass flutes made by Dutch flute-maker Jelle Hogenhuis have a thick PVC tube (and a built-in microphone) and they are much more affordable. These flutes are primarily meant for ensemble playing, and have mechanisms which, though much bigger, are similar to that of a regular flute.

Other sizes

There are many other flute sizes: the *soprano* in G, which sounds exactly an octave higher than the alto flute; the *treble flute* in E-flat; and the B-flat flute, which sounds a whole tone lower than the ordinary flute. Then there's the slightly lower-sounding *tenor flute* or *flûte d'amour*, an

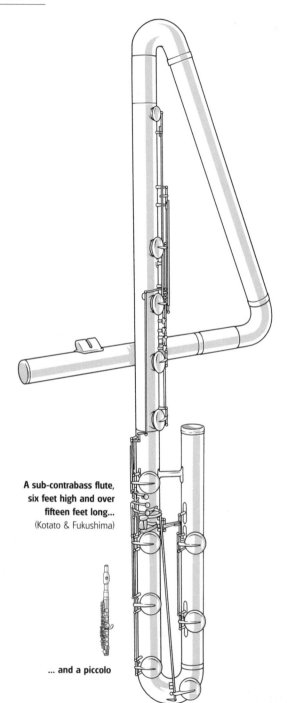

A sub-contrabass flute,
six feet high and over
fifteen feet long...
(Kotato & Fukushima)

... and a piccolo

instrument of an older design which is still made today. The names of the various flutes can be very confusing, especially if you travel abroad: what players in one country call a bass may be called a tenor or a contrabass somewhere else.

KEYLESS FLUTES

There are also many kinds of flutes without keys, such as the fife, which originated in the Middle Ages.

Fifes

Fifes are usually made of a single piece of metal and have no keys. Originally, the fife was always a very high-pitched instrument, but in modern fife and drum corps (see pages 119–120) other sizes are also known as 'fifes'. The highest-pitched is the descant, followed by the soprano, alto and tenor. Fifes are often made of metal with plastic tone holes, but you may also come across wooden or plastic models.

Tunings and names

Fifes come in different tunings. For instance, there are C, B, and B-flat sopranos. Incidentally, a soprano fife sounds as high as a piccolo, and the tenor fife in C is the same pitch as the 'ordinary' flute.

Children's flutes

Children sometimes learn to play on special keyless children's flutes. You can read more about these in Chapter 3.

WOODWIND INSTRUMENTS

The flute belongs to the woodwind family of instruments, even though it's now almost always made of metal. Here's a brief look at the other common members of this family.

Clarinet

A clarinet has a tube made of wood, or sometimes plastic, which is cylindrical for most of the way down. It has a key system that looks similar to the flute's, but it isn't quite the same. Some of the tone holes don't have keys, for example – you stop them directly with your fingers. The way you play the clarinet is very different as well. Attached to the

Three other woodwind instruments: a clarinet, an oboe and an alto saxophone

mouthpiece is a thin piece of reed, which vibrates to create the sound when you blow through the mouthpiece.

Saxophone

Though it's made of brass, the saxophone is a member of the woodwind family, not the brass family. This is because of its reed-blown mouthpiece (very similar to a clarinet's) and key system (similar to a flute's). The tube of a saxophone is conical: it gets steadily wider from the mouthpiece onwards. The alto and tenor saxophone are the two most common sizes, but there are others too.

Oboe and bassoon

The oboe has a conical tube, from narrow to wide, just like the sax. But in other ways it is more like a clarinet: it is made of wood and has both keys and open tone holes. Unlike either of these instruments, though, the oboe is a *double-reed instrument*, which means the sound is made by the vibration of two reeds against each other. The other common double-reed instrument is the bassoon, which is much larger and lower-sounding. The sax and the clarinet are both described as *single-reed instruments*.

Air-reed

While on most woodwind instruments you vibrate the air with a reed, on a flute you make vibrations by blowing against an edge. However, flute players sometimes refer to their *air-reed*.

10. HOW THEY'RE MADE

There are big factories which produce thousands of flutes per month and single-person workshops where only a few instruments are made each year. There are many differences between factory flutes and handmade ones, but in very general terms they're made in the same way.

Most factories and flute-makers don't produce every component of their instrument from scratch. The metal tube is often purchased from another manufacturer, for instance, as are the pads. And silver plating is often left to a specialized company.

Old and new
Flute-making is a very old craft, and there are flute-makers who still work in the same way as their predecessors from a hundred or more years ago. On the other hand, some modern factories use computers to design parts and computer-controlled machines to finish them to the nearest ten thousandth of an inch.

Drawn tone holes
Most flutes have drawn tone holes. To make them, small 'pilot' holes are drilled in the tube, and then a metal shaft called a *spike*, which is inset with steel balls or *bullets*, is inserted into the tube and pushed through the holes.

Drawn and finished
The metal which is forced upwards by the bullets forms the edge of a tone hole; this edge is finished by folding or rolling it (see page 53).

Soldered tone holes

On a flute with soldered tone holes, loose metal rings are soldered onto the tube, and only then are the actual holes drilled.

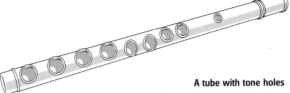

A tube with tone holes

Polished

When all the components have been extensively cleaned and polished the mechanism is fitted to the flute, and the positioning of everything is checked. After this, the flute is padded and adjusted.

The headjoint

Mouth holes are still generally cut by hand, except on cheaper flutes. The headjoint tube is precisely shaped on a mould, and the chimney and lip plate are soldered onto it.

Wood

The wood for a wooden flute or piccolo needs to dry for a long time before it's used. The longer it's dried, the smaller the risk that the instrument will later crack – some flute-makers use wood from trees cut down thirty or forty years ago, or even longer. A wooden flute starts life as a square-ended block which is turned into a cylindrical shape on a lathe. The inside is then drilled out and the wood finished. The ribs are attached with small screws.

By hand

Generally, the more you pay for a flute, the more work will have been done by hand and the more precise the construction will be. More money also usually buys you better quality control too – on expensive flutes, regular checks are made during the manufacturing process to make sure that everything is going to plan, and before they are shipped they are extensively tested and adjusted. Cheaper flutes are adjusted in the factory too, of course, but not as thoroughly, which is why they often need to be adjusted again before they play really well.

11. THE BRANDS

When you go to buy a flute, you are confronted with a whole range of brands – large and small, famous and obscure, budget and expensive. Here's a brief run-through of some of the famous and important.

The following nine companies – listed alphabetically, not in order of importance – are the biggest producers of flutes in the lower price ranges. However, many of them also make expensive professional instruments.

Armstrong® Established in 1931 by flute repairer William Armstrong, the American Armstrong brand has been part of United Musical Instruments (UMI) since 1985. The same company also incorporates manufacturers of trumpets (Conn), trombones (King) and clarinets (Artley). Armstrong supplies piccolos, C flutes and alto flutes.

 The French firm Buffet Crampon was set up in 1836. Later, members of this instrument-making family worked on improvements to the flute, and they adapted Boehm's keywork system for the clarinet. These days the brand's three flute series are made in Germany.

 Besides C flutes, piccolos, alto flutes and bass flutes, the US-based Emerson brand also makes instru-

ments in different tunings, such as flutes pitched in G and E-flat. Emerson is one of the few brands to make its own pads; these are also used by other manufacturers.

Gemeinhardt Kurt Gemeinhardt, who learned the craft of flute-making from his father, worked in Switzerland and later in the States, setting up his own firm in 1948. Of the factories which build only flutes, Gemeinhardt is the world's largest. Gemeinhardt also produces piccolos, alto flutes and bass flutes.

JUPITER Jupiter is a large Taiwanese company which makes all kinds of wind instruments, from trombones and trumpets to flutes. It is famous for its instruments designed especially for children and beginners, but it also produces the more expensive Di Medici series.

Pearl

The Japanese Pearl brand is well known for its drum kits as well as its flutes. The first Pearl flutes were made in the late 1960s, and soon afterwards a fully pinless mechanism was introduced. Like the other brands described here, Pearl is mainly active in the lower price categories, but the factory also makes solid gold flutes.

Selmer® Originally a French brand, Selmer is best known for the saxophones and clarinets which it still builds in France. Selmer flutes and piccolos are only made by its American subsidiary Selmer USA, which is one of the few brands which offer silver flutes with gold-plated mechanisms.

 The British clarinettist Trevor James sold his first handmade flutes in the late 1970s. In the early 1980s he became a partner in an Asian factory which since then has exclusively built C flutes, alto flutes and – starting a few years ago – saxophones for the TJJ brand. Final adjustments are made to the instruments in Britain.

⊛YAMAHA® The one-man organ factory started by Torakusu Yamaha in Japan in 1889 is now the world's largest manufacturer of musical instruments. Yamaha produces everything from bass flutes to piccolos, from drums to grand pianos and from trumpets to amplifiers and synthesizers – not to mention motorbikes, bathtubs, sailing boats and much more.

Other inexpensive brands

The brands listed above are not the only ones which build flutes in the lower price ranges. Other names you may come across include **Amati** (from the largest Czech wind instrument factory), **Hernals** and **Sun Haruno** from Japan, **Grassi** and **Orsi** from Italy, **Dixon** from Taiwan and the German **Mönnig** brand, which also makes wooden flutes, alto flutes and bass flutes. In addition, some importers and stores have their 'own' brands: often Asian-made flutes labelled with the store's name or a made-up name. Not all flute brands are available everywhere.

More expensive brands

There are also plenty of brands with price lists that start where those of the brands named above stop. Their cheapest flutes may cost around £2000/$3000 or more, and their most expensive models five or ten times that much. A few expensive Japanese brands are **Altus**, **Kotato & Fukushima**, **Mateki**, **Miyazawa**, **Muramatsu** (the first Japanese flute manufacturer), **Sankyo** and **Takezawa**. German makers include **Braun** (piccolos), **Lederer** and **Hammig**, incorporating both Philipp Hammig and the slightly more expensive August Richard Hammig brand. American high-end brands include **Burkart** and **Burkart-Phelan**, **Brannen** (optionally with Eva Kingma's key-on-key system; see page 49), **Haynes** (one of the first American manufacturers) and **Powell**. There are also many small, expensive brands in other countries, such as the Italian piccolo brand **Bulgheroni**.

Custom built

Besides these brands, most countries still have flute-makers who build their instruments entirely by hand. Such flutes can be made to your exact requirements, but naturally they're very expensive. It is a good deal more affordable to have only the headjoint made by hand, either in metal or one of many different types of wood – and there are more flute headjoint-makers around than flute-makers. They often advertise in the magazines listed in *Want To Know More?* (page 130).

12. GROUPS AND ORCHESTRAS

Flute players perform in symphony orchestras and in duos, in fife and drum corps and in bands which accompany singers and other musicians. You find them in wind quintets, in flute ensembles and in all kinds of other groups and orchestras. This chapter briefly describes these groups, the music they play and the role of the flute in them.

The biggest type of ensemble is the symphony orchestra, which consists of between fifty and a hundred musicians – sometimes even more. The violinists and viola players make up the biggest group; there are generally more than twenty of them in total. The flute section usually consists of two or three players, and if there are parts for piccolo or alto flute, they are normally played by the same people.

Blending and solos

In the symphony orchestra the flute has two main roles. First, it's a blending instrument, an instrument that gives the sound extra colour – you may not always be able to hear it, but you'd miss it if it wasn't there. Second, it's a melody instrument, an instrument which plays the tune. Sometimes all the flute players will play the melody together, and other times there will be a solo, usually performed by the 'first' or 'principal' flute player. Some large orchestras have a separate soloist for the piccolo.

The other musicians

As well as the flute section and the string players (violin, viola, cello, bass), symphony orchestras also have brass players (trumpet, trombone, tuba, French horn, etc), other woodwind players (clarinet, bassoon, oboe), percussionists (timpani, snare drum, cymbals, xylophone, etc) and a harpist.

Smaller ensembles

You can of course play classical music in smaller groups too. The chamber orchestra is a miniature version of the symphony orchestra, but a lot of music has been written for flute duos (two flutes), for flute together with guitar or harp, or for flute, piano and string instruments, to name just a few combinations. Another popular format is the wind quintet, which includes flute, clarinet, oboe, bassoon and French horn.

Only flutes

There are also groups which consist only of flute players. Generally, these groups focus on classical music, but their repertoires also often include arrangements of jazz, folk and pop tunes, and many other styles. These groups often use a combination of regular flutes, piccolos and alto flutes, but in the larger groups you also find bass and contrabass flutes, and sometimes flutes in other tunings and sizes.

Flute ensembles

Smaller flute-only groups, with no more than ten or fifteen musicians, are usually called flute ensembles. And even smaller groups are often named after the number of players – flute quartets and flute quintets, for example.

Flute orchestras

A flute orchestra may number fifty or even more players, and has a conductor. Some smaller groups without conductors also call themselves flute orchestras. Others – big and small – prefer to use the name flute choir.

WIND BANDS

As their name suggests, wind bands consist of wind instruments – usually with some added percussion. Here are some of the various types.

Fife and drum corps

Fife and drum corps are a type of ensemble found mostly

in military contexts. In many of these groups, the fifes have been replaced by flutes, piccolos, alto and bass flutes; other corps still use one-piece keyless instruments (see also page 109). A fife and drum corps may number around twenty musicians, but some have eighty or more members.

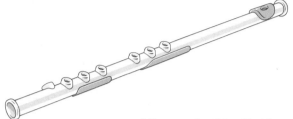

A fife: a one-piece flute without keys

Concert bands

A concert band is a wind band which consists mainly of brass and woodwind players, with clarinettists foremost among them, plus a number of percussionists. There are usually two flute players, though large bands sometimes have three or more.

Show bands

Though there is no fixed line-up, a show band generally consists of roughly the same instruments as a concert band – usually flute players are included. The difference is that show bands usually perform while marching, whether on stage, at sports events or parades.

Lessons and competitions

Bands often take part in local or national competitions, and many bands are affiliated with a music school or association, which may provide lessons, rehearsal space, and masterclasses.

JAZZ, ROCK AND MORE

As a flute player, you can also join all kinds of other groups and bands. Flutes are often used in folk, new-age and 'world' music, and in groups which accompany solo singers, choirs, operas and musicals. If you want to play styles like jazz, rock, Latin or rhythm 'n' blues, it's important that your flute is properly amplified. Get yourself a flute microphone (see pages 90–91) and that's no problem at all. In many of these bands the flute players are there to spice up the sound and give it some extra colour, but if you join a small jazz group you'll regularly play solos too. Jazz groups usually consist of a rhythm section (piano, bass, drums and sometimes guitar) and one or more wind players.

GLOSSARY AND INDEX

This glossary contains short definitions of all the flute-related terms used in this book. There are also some words you won't find in the previous pages, but which you might come across in magazines, catalogues and books. The numbers in brackets refer to the pages where the terms are used in this book.

Active keys *(96–97)* The keys which are open when you're not playing. The *inactive keys* (trill keys, G-sharp and D-sharp) are closed when you're not playing.

Air-reed *(111)* A flute doesn't have a real reed like a saxophone or clarinet, but flute players do sometimes talk about their *air-reeds*.

Allergies *(34, 73, 94–95)* The metal that a flute is made of or plated with may cause allergic reactions – nickel is especially problematic.

Alpaca See: *Nickel silver.*

Alternate fingerings *(47)* Almost every note can be played with one or more alternate fingerings as well as with the normal fingering.

Alto flute *(14–16, 57–58)* An alto flute is a longer and lower-sounding version of the 'standard' flute. See also: *Transposing instruments.*

Axis See: *Rods.*

B foot See: *Footjoint.*

Bass flute *(16–17, 57–58)* A bass flute is approximately twice as long as the standard Boehm flute, and it sounds one octave lower.

B-flat lever *(10)* Another name for the B-flat trill lever, which is also called the *Brossa B-flat*, after the inventor of this and other keys.

Blowing edge *(6)* You direct your airstream against the blowing edge, or *sounding edge*, of the mouth hole.

Body *(5)* Another word for the *middle joint* of a flute, or the longest section of a piccolo.

Boehm flute *(3)* One of the many names used to describe the 'standard' flute, this term is the name of the man who developed the modern flute, Theobald Boehm. His name is sometimes written Böhm, but he himself spelled it Boehm. See also: *Flute.*

Bore See: *Taper.*

Briccialdi B-flat *(105)* The B-flat lever which you operate with your left thumb. It is named after its inventor.

Brossa B-flat See: *B-flat lever.*

Brossa F-sharp *(54)*

C flute See: *Flute.*

C foot See: *Footjoint.*

C-arms See: *Y-arms.*

Case *(88–90)* A flute should always be stored and transported in a case.

Case cover *(88–90)* A cover for a flute case.

Chimney *(33, 34, 61)* The section between the lip plate and the tube. It's also known as the *riser*.

Cleaning rod *(9, 82, 83–84)* You dry the inside of

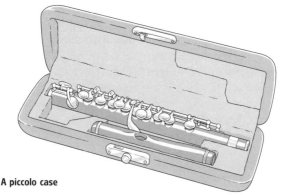

A piccolo case

your flute with a cloth wrapped around a cleaning rod. The notch in a cleaning rod can be used to check the position of the stopper.

Closed hole keys See: *Keys*.

Concert flute See: *Flute*.

Conical *(39, 103)* Wooden and plastic piccolos are conical: the tube gets steadily narrower towards the end. The flute has a cylindrical tube.

Cooper scale See: *Scale*.

Crown *(6, 63, 82)* The cap which closes off the top end of a headjoint.

C-sharp trill key See: *Trill keys*.

Cups *(63)* The actual keys or 'lids' which stop the tone holes. Also known as *pad cups* and *key cups*.

Curved headjoint *(14, 19, 58)* Children's flutes, alto flutes and bass flutes often have curved headjoints, also known as *U–shaped headjoints*.

Direct keys *(8)* The five keys that your fingers rest 'directly' on (A, G, F, E, D). On an open hole flute these are the open hole keys. The

other keys are described as the *indirect keys*.

Donut *(47–48)* On flutes without a split E, a donut can make the high E easier to play. See also: *Split E*.

Drawn tone holes See: *Tone holes*.

Duplicate G-sharp Another name for the lower G key.

E mechanism See: *Split E*.

Embouchure *(18)* This term describes the position of your mouth and everything around it that contributes to your sound. An *embouchure plate* is another term for lip plate, and an *embouchure hole* is a mouth hole.

Extruded tone holes See: *Tone holes*.

Fife *(1, 102, 109)* A type of transverse flute, usually without keys.

Flautist See: *Flutist*

Flute The term 'flute' can be used to describe any type of flute, but usually it implies the 'standard' modern instrument, as discussed in this book. Other names for 'standard' flute are Boehm flute (after its inventor), the C flute (because it's 'in C'), the soprano flute (to differentiate it from the alto or bass flutes), and concert flute.

Flutist In the US and various other countries the term flutist is used to describe a flute player. In Britain the word flautist is used instead.

Footjoint, foot *(5, 6, 51–52)* The bottom section of a flute. Most flutes have a *C foot*, but you can also get a *B foot*, which is slightly longer and allows the instrument to go a semitone (a halftone) lower.

French A 'French-style' flute has a *French mechanism* with open hole keys *(8)* – or *French pointed key arms (52)* – and an in-line G. A headjoint with a *French taper (59)* gives an elegant sound, and a French-style case *(88)* is a case without a handle.

G/A keys Another name for the two G keys.

G/A trill keys See: *Trill keys.*

German silver *(32)* See: *Nickel silver.*

Gizmo *(52)* Extra lever with which you can close the B

key of a B foot to make the high C (c''''') respond better.

Gold plating *(34, 101)* You can have any part of your flute plated with gold. This may be useful if your perspiration tarnishes silver, or if you have a nickel allergy.

Headjoint, head *(5–6, 32, 37, 56– 62, 73)* The 'top' part of a flute with the mouth hole in it.

Inactive keys See: *Active keys.*

Indirect keys See: *Direct keys.*

In–line G See: *Offset G.*

Insurance *(87–88)* You may be able to extend your home insurance to cover your flute.

Key cups See: *Cups.*

Key rods See: *Rods.*

Keys *(5–11, 48–51, 66)* You stop the tone holes of a flute using keys. On an *open hole flute* five of the keys have holes in them.

Keywork See: *Mechanism.*

Lever *(6, 8)* Some keys are closed or opened with a lever.

Lip plate *(5–6, 32–33, 34, 59–60, 94)* A metal head-joint always has a lip plate (also called a *mouth plate* or *embouchure plate*), which is attached to the headjoint by the *chimney*.

Mechanism *(5, 32–33, 40–43, 64)* The keys, rods, springs and levers which you use to close and open the tone holes. Also known as the *action*, *keywork*, *key mechanism* or *key system*.

Microphone *(90–91)* You can amplify a flute via a vocal microphone, a special flute microphone system or a headset.

Middle joint *(5–6)* The longest section of a flute, also known as the *body*.

Mouth hole *(5–6, 60–61)* To make a note, you direct your airstream at the *blowing edge* of the mouth hole.

Mouth plate See: *Lip plate*.

Nickel silver *(32)* Most silver-plated flutes are made of nickel silver, an alloy of copper, zinc, nickel and some other metals – but no silver. It's also known as German silver, white bronze or alpaca.

Offset G *(11, 45)* On a flute with an offset G, both G keys are positioned slightly further outwards (away from the player). This makes them easier to reach than if they are in line with the other keys, as on a 'French-style' flute with an *in-line G*.

Open hole keys, open hole flute See: *Keys*.

Overcut *(61)* The edges of an *overcut* mouth hole are cut away to make them slanted. On an *undercut* mouth hole, the corners between the mouth hole and tube are slanted.

Pad cups See: *Cups*.

Pads *(6, 43–44, 79, 97–100)* The thin, membrane-covered discs on the bottoms of the keys. A pad provides an airtight seal over a tone hole when a key is closed.

Padsaver *(85)* A long, fluffy plume which you can stick inside your flute after drying it to absorb any remaining moisture.

Perforated keys *(51)* Another name for open hole keys.

Piccolo *(12–14, 20, 37–40, 68)* A type of small flute. The piccolo is about half the size of a standard flute and sounds one octave higher.

Pillars See: *Posts.*

Pins, pinless mechanism *(42, 47)* Most flutes have small pins in the long rods of the mechanism, but some brands make pinless mechanisms.

Plateau style keys *(51)* Another name for closed hole keys.

Plugs *(50, 66)* You can temporarily or permanently block up the holes in open hole keys with plugs. See also: *Keys.*

Pointed key arms See: *French.*

Posts *(43)* The posts, or *pillars*, are the short metal supports that hold the rods of the mechanism at the right height above the body.

Range *(11–12)* The distance between the highest and lowest notes of a flute.

Reform lip plate *(60)* A plastic lip plate with large wings. See also: *Wings.*

Reverse B-flat/B *(55)* If you have a reverse B-flat/B, the keys by your left thumb

work the other way around.

Rhodium *(34)* Silver-coloured metal which is harder than gold. It is used as an alternative material for plating lip plates.

Ribs *(43)* The thin metal strips on the body of a flute that support the *posts*, which in turn hold the rods of the mechanism. Some metal piccolos and older flutes may be ribless, with the posts mounted directly onto (or into, in the case of a wooden instrument) the body. Ribs are also called *straps.*

Ring keys *(51, 103–105)* Another name for open hole keys.

Riser See: *Chimney.*

Rod-axles See: *Rods.*

Roller *(9, 10, 63)* Round 'lever' with which you operate the C key and, on a B foot, the key for the low B.

Scale *(66)* The scale of a flute refers to the exact position and size of the tone holes.

Secondhand buying tips *(28–29, 71–74)*

Soldered tone holes See: *Tone holes.*

Soprano flute See: *Flute*.

Sounding edge See: *Blowing edge*.

Split E *(46–48)* A mechanism which makes the high E (e''') easier to play. It's also called the *split E mechanism*, the *E mechanism* or the *split G* (because the arm of the mechanism 'splits' the two G keys, which are normally coupled). See also: *Donut*.

Split G See: *Split E*.

Springs *(9, 42)* The springs on a flute make sure the keys return to their proper positions after you have closed or opened them.

Steels See: *Rods*.

Stopper *(6, 62–63, 67–68, 81–83, 94)* Between the crown and the mouth hole is the stopper or *tuning cork*, which must be in exactly the right place if you are to play in tune. Stoppers are usually made of rubber, plastic or cork.

Strap See: *Rib*.

Strike wall See: *Blowing edge*.

Student flute A term used by some manufacturers to mean a either a beginner's flute or any non-professional model.

Taper *(59)* The taper of a flute usually refers to the profile of the headjoint, from narrow to wide. An alternative word is *bore*.

Tenons *(77–78)* The ends of a headjoint, body and footjoint which slide inside each other.

Tone holes *(5, 6, 53–54, 112–113)* Most flutes have sixteen tone holes. Usually these are 'drawn' or 'extruded' from the tube; on expensive flutes they may be soldered onto the tube.

Transposing instruments *(15–16)* The alto flute is a transposing instrument, which means the notes which you read and finger are different to the notes actually produced.

Traversa *(102)* The predecessor of the modern flute.

Trill keys *(8, 19, 54–55)* Special keys to make certain trills easier.

Tuning *(79–81)*

Tuning cork See: *Stopper*.

Undercut See: *Overcut*.

U-shaped headjoint See: *Curved headjoint.*

White bronze See: *Nickel silver.*

Winged embouchure *(59–60)* A lip plate with wings.

Y-arms *(53)* Most flutes have Y-arms on the keys, which are also called C-arms. Others have *pointed cup arms.*

WANT TO KNOW MORE?

This book provides all the information you need in order to buy, use and maintain a flute. If you want to know more there are hundreds of books, magazines and Web sites you could consult, from those which help players find a teacher, course or ensemble, to those about specific brands or products.

MAGAZINES

Every country has one or more organizations which arrange workshops, courses and fairs for flute players, and help flute players to get in touch with each other. Many of these organizations publish their own magazine.

- *Pan* is the magazine of the British Flute Society. You can subscribe on the BFS Web site (see next page).
- *Flutewise* is a quarterly magazine aimed primarily at the young. You can subscribe on the Flutewise Web site (see next page).
- You can find out about more international flute organizations and their magazines on the *Flutes are Fun!* Web site (see next page).

BOOKS

Countless books have been written about flutes. The list below includes several which discuss in greater depth the kinds of subjects covered by this book, as well as playing the flute and the flute repertoire.

- *The Flute Book – A Complete Guide for Students and Performers*, Nancy Toff (Oxford University Press, Oxford/New York, 1996; 493 pages; ISBN 0 19 510502

8). Nearly eighty pages are devoted to the development of the modern flute, maintenance and choosing a flute.

- *The Flute*, Raymond Meylan (Batsford, London, 1988; 143 pages; ISBN 0 7134 5737 6). A very readable book about the history of the flute, from the first instruments through the Renaissance and Baroque periods to the modern flute.
- *Flute*, James Galway (Yehudi Menuhin Music Guides; Kahn & Averill, London, 1990; 244 pages; ISBN 1 871082 13 7). As well as the subjects listed above, this book includes an enlightening chapter by Albert Cooper (see also page 66) on the construction of flutes and head-joints.
- *The Complete Guide to the Flute* by J. James Phelan offers a lot of technical information about maintenance, repair and construction. The book is temporarily out of print, but the full text is available as a special service for visitors to the Web site of flute-makers Burkart and Phelan (www.flute-makers.com). J. Phelan also made the video *Flute Fitness: Care and Easy Repair That You Can Do*, which covers troubleshooting, replacing corks and felts, cleaning and oiling.
- *How to Love Your Flute* – A Guide to Flutes and Flute Playing, Mark Shepard (Shepard Publications, 1999; 112 Pages; ISBN 0 938497 10 3). History, flute care and selection, and a variety of aspects of playing the instrument.

INTERNET

There are countless flute sites on the Internet, containing links, articles about flutes, lists of serial numbers, addresses of flute organizations and frequently asked questions. One of the best known and most informative sites is the one set up by Larry Krantz (Larry Krantz Flute Pages: users.uniserve. com/~lwk/welcome.htm). Here are some other good sites:

- World of Flutes (www.gwr.org/flutes)
- Flutes are Fun! (www.harpsong.org)
- Flutewise Online (www.flutewise.com)
- National Flute Association (www.nfaonline.org)
- The British Flute Society (www.bfs.org.uk)
- The Flute Network (www.flutenet.com)

ESSENTIAL DATA

In the event that your instrument is stolen or lost, or if you decide to sell it, it's always useful to have all the relevant details, including the serial number and original price, close at hand. You can jot this information down on these pages.

INSURANCE

Company:	
Phone:	Fax:
E-mail:	
Agent:	
Phone:	Fax:
E-mail:	
Premium:	
Policy number:	

FLUTE

Flute		
Brand and type:		
Serial number:		
Price:		
Date of purchase:		
Purchased from:		
Phone:	Fax:	
E-mail:		
Special characteristics:		
Split E:	yes	no
Keys:	open hole	closed hole
G keys:	in-line	offset

Other characteristics (silver plated, solid silver, wood or other materials, special trill keys, etc.):

PICCOLO

Brand and type:

Serial number:

Price:

Date of purchase:

Purchased from:

Phone: Fax:

E-mail:

Special characteristics:

ALTO FLUTE OR OTHER FLUTE

Brand and type:

Serial number:

Price:

Date of purchase:

Purchased from:

Phone: Fax:

E-mail:

Special characteristics:

ADDITIONAL NOTES

....
....
....
....
....
....
....
....
....
....
....
....
....
....
....
....
....
....
....
....
....
....
....
....
....
....
....
....
....
....
....
....

MUSIC ROUGH GUIDES ON CD

'Like the useful Rough Guide travel books and television shows, these discs delve right into the heart and soul of the region they explore'
– *Rhythm Music (USA)*

Available from book and record shops worldwide or order direct from World Music Network, Unit 6, 88 Clapham Park Road, London SW4 7BX
tel: 020 7498 5252 • fax: 020 7498 5353 • email: post@worldmusic.net

Hear samples from over 50 Rough Guide CDs at
WWW.WORLDMUSIC.NET

Will you have enough stories to tell your grandchildren?

©2001 Yahoo! Inc.

Yahoo! Travel

DO YOU
YAHOO!

ROUGH GUIDE
Music Guides

Music Reference Guides

Essential CD Guides

Mini Guides

"...attractively produced, competitively priced, meticulously
researched and interestingly written"
Peter French, The Bookseller

www.roughguides.com